TRIPOLI WITNESS

TRIPOLI WITNESS

RANA JAWAD

GILGAMESH
PUBLISHING LTD

Tripoli Witness

Published by Gilgamesh Publishing in 2011
Email: info@gilgamesh-publishing.co.uk
www.gilgamesh-publishing.co.uk

ISBN 978-1-908531-13-1

The Publishers would like to thank the BBC for their kind support in licensing the reproduction of the Tripoli Witness blogs which appear on pp139-205 of this book

Printed and bound by CPI Group (UK) Ltd., Croydon, CR0 4YY

CIP Data: A catalogue for this book is available from the British Library

CONTENTS

ACKNOWLEDGMENTS

I want to thank my husband, Motaz Elgheriani, for being patient and supportive at a time when I needed it the most, for reminding me of many details as I worked through the book and for being an invaluable source of newsgathering during the siege in Tripoli. *Tripoli Witness* would have had much less to say if it were not for his eyes and ears.

To my father, who relentlessly encouraged me at times when I had no will to stay another day in Gaddafi's Libya, who silently accepted my long absences at a time when he needed to see me the most when he was ill – I could not have done it without you. To my mother, who laughed and cried with me for many years, who stood waiting at the door for every annual visit with a large spread of my favourite things – your strength is inspiring.

I need to thank the *BBC African Service* for believing in me at a time when few would have given a young journalist the time of day. I probably would not have moved to Libya as a correspondent if it were not for this invaluable programme in the *BBC World Service*. It had the foresight of recognizing the importance of covering Libya at a time when few could. I am grateful for that, and my bosses' patience in listening to my long rants on the phone and reading my even longer emails at times of great frustration in reporting under a dictatorship for many years. Their support never wavered during the uprising either. My editors and bosses, Josephine Hazeley, Stephane Mayoux, Solomon Mugera, and my fellow colleagues at the African Service, and BBC Online – thank you. I also wish to thank Paul Danahar, our Middle East bureau chief for encouraging the birth of what was to become *Tripoli Witness* during the Libyan uprising and for being there at the other end of the line when I needed him to be. This book would not have made as much sense if it were not for the keen editing eyes of my colleague Paul Kenyon who also championed my need to write it.

My mother-in-law kept me sane for many long months during the difficult period that many residents in the capital lived through and her input on life in Benghazi was paramount to my understanding of the birthplace of the popular uprising. I have made many invaluable friends in Tripoli over the years, all of whom contributed to my love of this country and the information I gathered for BBC Online in the first four months of the revolution. For this and much more I must thank Afaf, Sabrina, Mysoun, Najat, Sherif, Anas, Siraj, and Mohamed. The list is longer and the rest know who they are.

FOREWORD

BY

PAUL KENYON

Paul Kenyon is an award winning BBC journalist who was the first to report from both sides of the Libyan conflict in 2011. He was the Royal Television Society's specialist reporter of the year in 2010 for his documentaries on the fate of African migrants who attempted to pass through Libya en route to Europe. He filmed in Libya several times during the Gaddafi regime and has reported from around the world for the BBC's Panorama programme for more than a decade.

When Gaddafi was still in power, it once took me more than a year to secure a visa to report from Libya. The names of officials seemed to change from one week to the next. I wrote to one of the country's former Prime Ministers, I drank mint tea with officials at the Libyan People's Bureau in London, I attended celebrations for Gaddafi's revolution at a swanky hotel in Mayfair. But my requests never even received an acknowledgement. Then, as was typical with Libya at the time, I received a phone call late at night. "You can come this weekend, no later". I knew if I asked for a different date, I may never get the chance again.

Each filming trip after that was two to three weeks long, and the Libyans were experts at bleeding time away so the least possible could be achieved.

Government minders were obligatory. No camera could be turned on without their permission. I once asked simply if we could film a street in the centre of Tripoli. "Who would you like me to ask on your behalf?" said the minder, "either Mr Ali or Mr Mohammed?" I had no idea who either person was, so I responded that he, the minder, should choose.

"No, you must choose, it must be one or the other" he said.

"Okay, I will go for Mr Ali"

"Oh dear" he smiled, "Mr Ali is on holiday and cannot be disturbed, not by anyone."

"Okay, just phone Mr Mohammed, and ask him." I responded, becoming exasperated.

The minder smiled more broadly this time. "Mr Mohammed can only give permission if his boss agrees" he said.

"Who's his boss?" I replied.

"...his boss is Mr Ali, and he's on holiday."

To achieve anything journalistic in Libya meant enduring a merry-go-round of mind games. Breaking the rules was pointless. They would simply take all your tapes and kick you out of the country. So, you had little choice but to conform.

As a foreign journalist, once back in London I could report what I wanted. The only punishment available to the regime was to block any prospect of me returning. However, for the BBC's Rana Jawad, a reporter who's actually based in Libya, the possible recriminations for a critical piece were far-reaching.

Every day she walked through a wilderness of smoke and mirrors, attempting to report on a regime which wanted to keep its activities secret. It was a country of torture and random imprisonment, of secret police and brutal decrees, a country governed by one of the most eccentric and unpredictable dictators of modern times. All rich territory for a journalist, but the line she had to walk was a fine one. Poke them too much and she'd be thrown out, poke them too little and there was no point in being there. Most of the time, Rana did just enough to make them cross – she poked them to the edge without tipping them over.

In April 2011, when I arrived in Tripoli during the uprising, a BBC team had just been arrested at a checkpoint. They were held in jail, and subjected to a mock execution. Other journalists were detained for weeks. One Friday, a group of us tried to shake off our minders, and travel to a part of town where a protest had been brutally put down. Within an hour, we were picked up by Gaddafi's secret police, bundled into minibuses, and returned to the hotel. It was an almost impossible task to find out the truth about what was happening in the City.

During that time Rana Jawad was separate from the rest of the press. She lived across the divide, in a place we couldn't visit, a place which still hadn't been liberated. Filing her reports under an assumed identity on the internet, she kept the world informed of what was happening as Gaddafi first of all clamped down and then gradually lost grip on Tripoli. Under the by-line Tripoli Witness, she brought us a fascinating story of lives and events which would otherwise have gone unreported. Over three months she continued to write, despite the constant threat that Gaddafi's secret police would raid her home and take her away.

This book contains the full collection of her Tripoli Witness articles, as well as Rana's reflections on being the BBC's reporter in Tripoli for seven years.

P.K.

London, November 2011

INTRODUCTION

In May, when asked if I was interested in authoring a book on Libya, I promptly thanked my publisher for inquiring and promised to get back to him soon. Like a snail detecting danger, I retreated. At the time I was still working "undercover" – a term I remain uncomfortable with because Tripoli Witness felt like an exposed, almost naked being that – with zero acrobatic skills – was performing at the Cirque du Soleil. It was a time when the accounts and reflections on the muted events, cries and thoughts of the city's residents were coming to an end due to further worries over personal security. A time when technology felt like a spy within the confines of the home I spent much of my time in for 6 months. Above all, it was a place that inevitably made me question where I would "hide" the manuscript's pages as it was being written.

On June 24th, I informed my publisher to-be that I was in a bad place, mentally and physically, and would not be able to work on anything. He gracefully signalled that he understood and would wait till the time was right.

It is now November 2011 and Colonel Gaddafi is dead, as is his son Mutassim Gaddafi, the former national security advisor to the regime. The images of Muammar Gaddafi's capture by fighters who arguably spent the better part of eight months fantasizing about the day they would catch him have caused a stir in the West. It is not entirely clear whether he was summarily executed or if he was killed in the cross-fire. There are many calls from human rights watchdogs and some in the West for an investigation to determine if a war crime has been committed by forces loyal to the National Transitional Council. His once heir-apparent to power, son, Saif Al-Islam

Gaddafi, was captured trying to flee the country on November 19th, and at the time of writing is being held by the Zintan brigade in the west of Libya. The International Criminal Court (ICC), which has a warrant for his arrest, has accepted that Saif Al-Islam will be tried on Libyan soil and not at The Hague. An investigation by the ICC's chief prosecutor, Luis Moreno-Ocampo, followed a referral in February by the UN security council that had unanimously adopted Resolution 1970 condemning the use of lethal force by the regime of Gaddafi against protesters.

Colonel Gaddafi was probably killed by the fighters who captured him. It was an undignified end to the life of a leader that stripped many here of their dignity during his decades of rule. He was once wanted by the Libyan population at large for being the dictator that he was for more than four decades, for the lives that he and his henchman destroyed in that time, and the misery they bestowed on many of the Libyan people's lives before and after the uprising. Saif Al-Islam's role in suppressing the uprising is without question; most Libyans are convinced he was a key player and feel that it is not a question of whether he is guilty or not, but when the guilty verdict will be handed down. His trial is expected to lay much to rest within a population seeking closure on his father's brutal regime. For many, anything less than a death sentence will not suffice.

Though the Colonel's other living sons are not wanted by the ICC, they are also wanted by the Libyan people for various serious and deadly offences, including their extraordinary abuse of state funds, and their callousness towards their fellow countrymen and women.

The late Mutassim Gaddafi was also probably spared from facing justice in the United States for his appalling choice of wardrobe when, on an official visit there as Libya's security advisor not long ago, he boldly faced photographers with the US secretary of State Hillary Clinton in a shiny brown suit.

I never believed Colonel Gaddafi or his sons would have their day in court because it was quite clear that if they were caught here they would be killed on site. Those claiming "shock" or indignation over the gruesome scenes of Gaddafi's last day alive may have been in serious denial over the facts on the ground. The fact is that many of those who took up arms against the regime either had a relative, a sibling or entire family killed during the military onslaught unleashed by the Gaddafi brigades in the early months of the uprising – before and after they took up arms. Others who fought against him simply abhorred the state, Gaddafi and the people they became under his rule. All in all, the chances of surviving a capture at the hands of the new brigades formed during the war were well below zero. It may seem inhumane or politically and legally unacceptable to an outside observer and even to some within Libya itself for various reasons – and in part it was. To many Libyans however, it was justice and peace; he was not an "average" person, he was the embodiment of all that most Libyans despised in their lives. He was their dictator. Over the months, I had heard many speak of what they would like to do to all of the Gaddafis; the scenarios they painted seemed like they were taken from some of the most gruesome horror movies of our time, with the added desire for mass public humiliation. It is a fate that was inflicted on thousands of Libyans over the decades.

You will find that the following pages will – in large part – often be void of specific dates and names; they are only used when necessary. This book is a reflection on many elements and realities constructed or influenced by Colonel Gaddafi's regime that will shed light on what led to the peaceful uprising in Libya that rapidly transformed into a bloody conflict to topple the man who ruled there for forty-two years. It is written through my own experiences and through the eyes and words of the people I have met and some of whom I have come to love in the seven years I have worked here as the BBC correspondent. This is also in large part a collection of the works of the elusive Tripoli Witness, a male alter-ego developed for BBC online in late February when I worked undercover in the capital during the first three months of the uprising. Above all, it is a tribute to the extraordinarily determined people of this country who for many decades came to be viewed as complacent, and socially and politically inept. Regardless of what may come and the divisions and hardship that may arise in a Libya without the "guide and leader of the 1969 revolution", the events have taken many by surprise, not least Colonel Gaddafi and his entourage who seemingly once believed they would be in power for eternity and beyond.

On April 1st, months after the departure of the Tunisian president Zine Al-Abidine Ben Ali from power and six weeks into the Libyan uprising, I came across a news report on television about Tunisia. It was yet another large protest in the Casaba area, at the gates of the old city.

The clip that followed showed an elderly Tunisian woman shouting at the camera, telling the audience that her son was kidnapped and tortured for seven days and that the secret police was still very much active in the country.

Questions invariably arise at this stage.

How do you undo decades of policing? How do you erase the knowledge of thousands of civil servants or civilians who suffered at the hands of a dictatorship – all of whom have only known the brutal measures they have grown accustomed to unleashing on their fellow countrymen and women? Have some African and Arab leaders ruled their countries for so long that they have destroyed any prospect for the formation of democratic governance?

The unfortunate reality – and some may argue pessimistic view – is that they possibly have or had. These are the wider questions that will be answered with time. As the Egyptian revolution drew to a close in February 2011, I recall arguing – with friends – that very little would change there due to the powers at play in the Middle East and Egypt's crucial role there; its relationship with Israel and US interests in maintaining the status quo of Cairo's friendly ties with Tel Aviv. This was perhaps a short-sighted argument because Egypt need not be ruled by a dictator to impose a relationship or decision that is unpopular with its people whilst simultaneously addressing the population's basic demands and rights; western governments do it all the time!

Tunisia, I felt, had a better chance at radical change given that the world at large does not really care about it – with the exception of the French, for historical colonial reasons and for its mutually beneficial trade in the textile industry. To the rest, it is quite simply a holiday hot-spot on the Mediterranean coastline.

As for Libya, anything in the absence of Muammar Gaddafi is seen by Libyans as a massive achievement, even a thoughtful song or a powerful sentimental poem that is politically driven. Unlike its neighbours, the population was long deprived of maturing on any strata. We are likely to hear of contentment for many years to come regardless of the outcome of its revolution in the long-term – unless it suddenly witnesses a complete breakdown in law and order and the birth of severe regional divisions, an insurgency, or if the budding rivalry between powerful brigades that formed during the conflict is not addressed immediately. Power needs to be centralized, militarily and politically, to allow the country to peacefully transition into what many hope will be a "democracy", however loosely we must use that term.

I do not know if long-serving dictators in the Arab world or in Africa have damaged any iota of hope or possibility for the changes that populations that suffered under their rule are striving for, or may fight for in the future. What can be said, however, is that there is no excuse for dictatorial policies in which unspeakable corruption and violations of the most basic of rights are rife. There is no excuse for clinging to power at any cost – not least at the expense of the blood of your fellow countrymen.

R.J.

CHAPTER ONE

A SHORT GUIDE TO GADDAFI'S LIBYA

Structure of security apparatus in Gaddafi's Libya

Every tyrant of our times, and for generations and millennia past, required a formidable security network to remain in power. There were the Praetorian and Varangian Guards of the Roman Empire, Mao Zedong's Red Guards, and Stalin's NKVD. Imagine a combination of them all, and it will give you some idea of Libya's complex and brutal security apparatus under Gaddafi.

It is tempting to include Mossad and the CIA in a wider list when considering Libya's intelligence arm, but I firmly believe that the country's intelligence and death squad communities were not nearly as bright, discreet or efficient.

Abdullah Al-Senussi is a name that most in Libya will never forget. He is a slightly pudgy and rather scary looking man of Chadian origin and he was the chief of at least two of Libya's intelligence organisations. He was married to Gaddafi's sister-in-law – though at times it seemed he was actually married to the Colonel himself. In 1989, French courts convicted him and five other Libyan officials in absentia for the 1984 bombing of the UTA airliner over Niger – an episode apparently forgotten after the Libyan regime financially and diplomatically settled the matter in

2004. He was once also accused of plotting to assassinate Saudi Arabia's Crown Prince Abdullah. That too was denied by the Libyan authorities in a hurried news conference in Tripoli in 2004.

To many Libyans, Mr Al-Senussi was the "devil incarnate" – the bogeyman in their nightmares and a pain in their toes. His name was enough to instil fear because not only did he oversee the internal security apparatus and military intelligence, he was a key figure behind some of the worst atrocities committed by the Gaddafi regime.

I was often told "he whom the intelligence community backs is he who shall rule Libya in the future" during discussions about who would succeed Gaddafi. Before the Libyan uprising, Abdullah Al-Senussi was a staunch ally of Saif Al-Islam Gaddafi, the leader's son widely touted as heir apparent.

As the popular revolt unfolded, at least one official who defected from Libya's dilapidated air force claimed Abdullah Al-Senussi ordered him to bombard Benghazi. He was also accused of playing a crucial role in the killing of protestors, as well as the recruitment of foreign mercenaries from neighbouring sub-Saharan countries who fought alongside Gaddafi's forces.

Abdullah Al-Senussi's fate is unknown at this time, though he is wanted by the International Criminal Court for alleged war crimes. At the time of writing, the latest rumour is that he has been captured in the city of Sabha. Although some officials confirmed this at the time, days later, the interim Prime Minister Adburrahim Al-Keeb said he had no confirmation he was in custody.

The Revolutionary Committee Movement

Otherwise known in Arabic as the *Lijan Thawriyah*, it was made up of tens of thousands of individual members. Each City and town contained a building which acted as their headquarters. Anyone could join, as long as they pledged allegiance to protect the ideals of the 1969 revolution which brought Colonel Gaddafi to power, and to his unfathomable structure of governance encompassed in the Green Book.

They received benefits unavailable to the average Libyan and some possessed a licensed firearm. However, it all depended on how much the higher powers trusted each member; the greater the trust the greater the benefits. This was one of the most reviled and feared networks of spies, informants, "thinkers", and executioners in the country. Some of its senior members were surprisingly well spoken and very well educated. It resembled a political party, but Libya was a single party state, and so the Revolutionary Committee Movement (RCM) was better described as a movement, and many of Libya's high ranking officials were aligned to it.

On February 16th 2011 at around 4:30 in the morning, Libya's state television channel Al-Jamahiriyah – which no longer exists today – broadcasted live pictures of men driving through Benghazi's streets waving and kissing posters of Colonel Gaddafi. These men were the regime's Revolutionary Committee members in the city. This was the state's way of refuting claims of protests in Benghazi where anti-Gaddafi chants had been heard. There was no presenter explaining the pictures or even why the channel was showing them. They were just there, with a caption on the side of the screen saying "Benghazi Live". In the old Libya, this kind of broadcast was a clear message from the state, to say "we are everywhere and we will overshadow you".

I have met and interviewed many members of the Revolutionary Committee Movement – it is invariably an unpleasant and at times chilling experience. There is one meeting I recall with a man called Mustafa Al-Zaidi. He was a plastic surgeon and once the foreign affairs coordinator of the RCM. Reporters usually aim to record no more than 10 minutes on tape for a story they are working on – in this case it ran to roughly one hour and ten minutes. The situation transformed into the interviewee lecturing the interviewer on the subject of Gaddafi's *Third Way*. It ended in something like an argument, which was perhaps unwise on my part. This was an exchange which never made it to air – the man simply never answered any of my questions, but successfully induced a splitting headache for the rest of the day.

A sub-group of the Revolutionary Committees was the Revolutionary or Republican guards. Their mission was to protect the ideals of Gaddafi's *Al Fateh revolution*, make arrests, and take people into questioning as well as sentencing the accused on the spot when necessary. They were mainly active in the 1980s.

Yet another sub-group was the Cleansing or Sterilization Committee known as *Lijan Tatheer*. It was namely tasked with implementing the *Min ayna laka hatha* decree which literally translated as "Where did thou acquire this from?" It was an ad hoc law alluding to the amassed wealth of Libyans; it allowed the state to dig into their bank accounts, records of assets, and businesses. This included indiscriminately stripping Libya's rich or moderately well-off population of their assets or businesses only to make others who were closer to the regime richer.

Money is power and Libyans who were seen as a potential threat to the Colonel's rule were prevented from acquiring wealth. Many Libyans resorted to opening accounts abroad or hiding their money at home.

Internal Security

Run by Abdullah Al-Senussi, this was known as the division largely responsible for the "dirty business" of the country. It too had a vast and complex network of sub-divisions tasked with overseeing various security matters. Some of its branches dealt largely with imprisonment and prison facilities. Internal Security was the most feared organisation after the RCM, though it was a closely run thing.

The External Security Service

Also known as foreign intelligence, The External Security Service was for many years headed by Musa Kusa, the man who later defected from Gaddafi's regime just a few weeks into the uprising. By that time he was foreign minister, and the man who had filled his place in External Security was Abu Zeid Dorda, the former governor of Misrata, once Secretary of planning and housing, and an ex-prime minister of Libya.

External intelligence officers did not necessarily focus their efforts on the outside; they were mostly tasked with monitoring Libyans both inside the country and abroad who had any dealings, meetings or barbecues with foreigners – especially foreign diplomats. They monitored emails, phone calls, the internet at large, embassies, Libyan visitors to foreign embassies and possibly people's luncheons, dinners, and trips to the toilet.

Surprisingly, many of them turned out to have only a shallow allegiance to the regime, and defected in large numbers during the uprising. Perhaps it was the day-to-day dealings with foreign intelligence agencies which had turned their backs on the Colonel.

Civil Guards

Locally known as *Haras Shaabi*, they were volunteers tasked with "defending" and providing ad hoc security to the people inside Libya's towns and cities. They would also join the brigade forces when necessary. Most of those involved were civil servants. The organisation came into its own during the uprising. Many of its members joined Gaddafi's brigades, and it is believed they took heavy losses on the frontlines. It was claimed by some that the trained brigade forces stayed well away from the intense fighting, and instead pushed the largely untrained civil guards to the front.

On a local level, they were the young men who manned Tripoli's checkpoints when the city was choked with security units as fighting spread across the rest of the country. They were generally despised by most people and seen as the primary suspects for the widespread looting of abandoned expat homes and foreign company headquarters whilst Tripoli was under siege.

Taxi Drivers and Miscellaneous Informants

It is no secret that many of Libya's taxi drivers worked for one security outfit or another. This was especially the case in the Libyan capital, where they were widely available, unlike other cities and towns in the country where civilians often acted as taxi drivers with their private cars. One had only to drive or walk past a security building in the early hours to realize that all the cars parked outside were the black and white vehicles that were (and still are) Libya's taxis. It was an amusing sight to say the least, if only for its depressingly obvious message. Immediately after Tripoli fell, the capital's taxis were depleted by more than half.

Others who willingly acted as informants for Gaddafi's regime included a neighbour, a friend, a relative or even a spouse. At times it was the dodgy looking man with a car rental service, the local baker, the neighbourhood tobacco salesman (who may or may not have been Tunisian) – the list of possibilities was endless.

This country has a population of roughly 6.5 million people. When people claimed half of Libya worked for security, they were only slightly exaggerating.

Gaddafi's Clan

In the last decade it is widely believed that Colonel Gaddafi's seven sons and one daughter were squandering state funds like never before, and dividing up the county's towns and cities in anticipation of their father's death. Videos began appearing on YouTube of their lavish lifestyles: private concerts, parties on luxury yachts, and in exotic nightclubs in European capitals. The state responded by blocking the video-sharing site in late January 2010. It did not really matter; the site was still being easily accessed via proxy-servers, or a simple, quick change in the IP address. The move was rendered even more useless in my eyes when a civil servant from Libya's telecom's company

LTT, the only ADSL internet provider in the country – run by Gaddafi's eldest son – offered me the "secret" IP address when I quizzed him over the matter off the record.

"It's not really us who blocked it" he said, before silently mouthing and gesturing with a finger pointing upwards to say the order came from...

"God?" I joked.

He nervously laughed. Naturally, he was pointing to Gaddafi as we sat in a large conference room at LTT's headquarters.

Gaddafi's Children

Mohamed reigned over the telecommunications sector and headed the Olympic committee. I am personally on the fence about him. He is an amicable, though reserved character – at least he appeared to be when I interviewed him on about three occasions. He is Colonel Gaddafi's oldest son, from his first wife – a former teacher. My landlord in Tripoli once told me "Mohamed is disciplined, his mother brought him up well because she is a teacher and a disciplinarian – he has manners, he did not grow up like the rest of his brothers amidst Gaddafi and his henchmen...the others were raised with a Bedouin, war-like mentality."

Many Libyans appeared to favour Mohamed because he seemed politically apathetic. However, he led one of the country's most vital sectors, a position he would not have held had he not been the son of Gaddafi. Many Libyans, and myself, expected him to defect from the regime – or at the very least simply run away and seek refuge abroad without commentary. The longer he remained during the conflict, the more people grew to resent him. Today he is not seen as the "good child", but simply a man who benefited greatly from his father's rule.

Saif Al-Islam Gaddafi quite clearly appeared to want it all; he was pegged as the heir-apparent to power. Unlike some of his brothers he led a discreet private life; you will not find photos or videos of him partying in Europe's most exclusive resorts. However, he has reportedly celebrated at least two birthdays in Montenegro with some ostentatious VIP's. For many years, Libyans appeared resigned to the idea that the Montenegro-loving son of Gaddafi would simply take over in the event of his father's death. Some were even looking forward to it, if only because he presented a reformist front and a younger face. He arguably became the second most hated man in Libya as the uprising unfolded for many reasons which you will discover in the coming pages. He played a leading role in the financial settlement over the bombing of the Pan Am flight over Lockerbie in Scotland in 1988, which Libya "accepted responsibility for" whilst simultaneously denying it was involved. Two hundred and seventy people died, mostly Americans.

Saif Al-Islam once spoke of his vision for a reformed Libyan media that resembled the BBC – obviously a preposterous suggestion in a police state. He arguably threw as many hissy fits as his father. In 2006, one of his close aides anonymously told the media that Saif was "leaving the country to work for an international economic organization abroad". In 2008 he declared "I'm leaving politics" – though he had no official role to leave in the first place. A short time later the "Libyan youth demonstrated" in praise of the Colonel and his son and demanded that Saif return to "active duty" in the country – the job he officially did not have.

In retrospect, his comments mirrored his father's oratory gibberish; he deflected blame onto others for his failed plans – a well established practice mastered by his father, and there was an attempt to create a cult-like following for him through his annual public addresses to "the youth". Though he was not a "thinker" like Muammar Gaddafi, he was a "painter". The signs of a dictator in-the-making were there for all to see, but still Libyans thought him the "reformist son" who was widely applauded in the West.

Mutassim once commandeered his own militia and was almost hunted down by his father at least once when he tried to breach the Bab Al-Aziziyah compound in Tripoli by force. The move was later rumoured to be a coup attempt, though no one is really sure of anything except that he fled the country for a short time whilst tempers cooled. He wanted the military power, and was always known as a vengeful, bloodthirsty character by Libyans. He last served as the country's National Security Advisor.

Hannibal almost monopolized the shipping industry and had long greasy hair. He married the Lebanese ex-lingerie model, Aline Skaff. He was arrested or "warned" to behave by authorities once or twice for allegedly beating her up in Europe's finest hotel rooms and wrecking the plush rooms in the process. In 2008, he and his wife were both arrested after being accused of abusing two members of their personal staff in Switzerland. This inevitably led to an almost never-ending spat between Libya and the neutral, docile state in Northern

Europe. The Swiss made a swift exit from Libya at the time, taking all their chocolate with them. The EU was dragged into the tit-for-tat game that ensued. Two Swiss businessmen were held in Tripoli for over a year on what many privately believed were trumped up charges. Switzerland eventually issued a travel blacklist with 188 high-profile names, including the Colonel. Since the Swiss are part of Europe's border-free Schengen zone, those on the list could no longer travel to other European nations either. Libya responded by banning Libyan visas to anyone living in Europe's Schengen zone. That affected 25 countries. It was imposed overnight. Even the Maltese – their best friends – could not get in. The matter was finally resolved in March 2010, less than a year before the country took up arms to depose the colonel.

Saadi – the not so talented professional footballer for many years – abandoned the pitch and dreamt of creating his own free trade zone – a Monte Carlo in Libya. The project he imagined was to stretch from the Western city of Zuwara near the Tunisian border and on towards Tripoli for about 60 kms along the coast and 30 kms inland. His little state would be headed by him and would have its own set of laws, courts and police force. It was surprisingly not financially endorsed by the state and was shelved. I do not know why. The widespread theory was that Saif Al-Islam would not allow it. Saadi complained to the media about the government's "prolonging of the process" a few years later, when he re-announced his plan for the free trade zone of something one might almost call Monte Libya.

He will perhaps forever be remembered as the son who comically suggested that he rule Benghazi in the midst of the second day of deadly protests during the uprising against his father in 2011. He made the announcement through a local radio station in Benghazi and fled about 24hrs later as the last garrison there was breached by the angry mob.

Little is known of **Khamis** except that he led a fierce brigade throughout the Libyan conflict and he received his military training at an academy in Moscow. In Tripoli his men were feared on an almost mythical level. They participated in capturing people they suspected of being opponents to the regime and severely beat them in the process. Then they took them to detention centres. On the frontlines of the conflict, his forces were believed to be largely responsible for some of the worst indiscriminate shelling in various Libyan cities.

Saif Al-Arab is an even more obscure son. He is said to have been religious at one point in his life and owned a very expensive house in Germany where he had been studying shortly before the uprising.

Aisha is Gaddafi's only daughter from his second wife Safia. She was seen as being dim and rather silly, but she was also tall and pretty. She once proudly and briefly joined Saddam Hussein's defence team. Some Libyans believe it was short-lived because her team probably realized she was not a real lawyer and would have never graduated with a degree if she were not "the daughter". "She was dim-witted in class" a state school teacher once told me. In her favour she led a charity foundation of her own that dealt with issues such as the abuse of women. She also owned a very opulent house, dubbed a "palace" by the media, in Arada street just off the up-market neighbourhood of Ben-Ashur in central Tripoli. Libyans stormed her home after the fall of Tripoli and found a golden mermaid cradling a chaise longue at the epicentre of the house, beneath the winding stairs. It simply screamed "kitsch" and "photo-op" for the families that poured in for a quick peek. Some young men did not leave before taking a swim in her rather large indoor swimming pool. She made several long public addresses in support of her father during the uprising – the last one was from her father's barracks.

Hanna is a mystery no more. Colonel Gaddafi's adopted daughter who was supposedly killed by the 1986 US bombardment of Libya was always known to be very much alive amongst Libyans. This was one of the first revealing pieces of information I came across from a very well-informed friend after I moved to Libya. The other was that there was no hope that I would be able to uncover the truth because unless it was privately relayed, it was simply not discussed. She is a doctor. The regime spread a rumour that it was not the same daughter who was killed in the bombing. People said it wasn't uncommon for another child to be named after a deceased one. I am 99.9% certain she is the same Hanna claimed to have died long ago. There are students who attended university with her in Tripoli and there are professionals in the medical industry who worked alongside her. Everyone knew who she was but feared for their lives if they were to speak of the matter openly. What I am unsure of is whether she is adopted or actually his child from another woman as many here believe.

Location, Location, Location

At the end of the nine month conflict in Libya that toppled and killed Colonel Gaddafi, some of his sons met a similar fate, whilst others remain physically unscathed but are probably mentally tormented as they consider their future.

In the early months of the conflict, Saif Al-Arab was believed to have been killed in a Nato airstrike in Tripoli targeting one of Gaddafi's family homes constructed of reinforced concrete. Conspiracy theories remain rife amongst Libyans pondering his fate. Some strongly believe he was executed by one of his brothers or his father for opposing the regime's handling of the protests.

Khamis was killed somewhere in the desert when his convoy was hit by a missile.

Mutassim is dead. He was alive in a video after his capture, seen drinking water from a bottle handed to him by his captors. His body was then seen lying in a meat freezer in Misrata alongside that of his father.

Mohamed, Hannibal and Aisha fled to Algeria a few weeks after Tripoli fell and Saadi fled to Niger. At the time of writing, they are all still free although Libya's new authorities have repeatedly requested their extradition. If that succeeds, many Libyans hope they will be put on trial for some of the numerous offences they are believed to have committed against the state and the people of Libya. Meanwhile, in November 2011, Saif Al-Islam was captured in Libya. He has since been kept in a secret location near the mountainous town of Zintan.

Under Gaddafi's dictatorship, the courts here came to be viewed with disdain by Libyans who were long persecuted by them, with what most believed was flawed or fabricated evidence. The Libyan judiciary was ultimately a tool of repression and injustice. Saif Al-Islam's case will be the first of its kind to be prosecuted in the country. This is uncharted territory for Libya's new authorities and the judicial system, although there is no shortage of lawyers and judges who know what the law is. The test will be how the law is used under the banner of a new beginning.

The Third Way: Colonel Gaddafi's Green Book

The Green Book's rules of governance, in all their nonsensical glory, were adopted in 1977 following a declaration issued in the desert city of Sebha. With that came a new title – not name – for the country: *The Socialist People's Libyan Arab Jamahiriya*.

This was a time when so-called "direct popular democracy" was implemented, when the *Jamahiriyah* or "state of the masses" would rule itself. It is unclear when, but this was later tweaked to *The Great Socialist People's Libyan Arab Jamahiriya*.

I encourage you to Google the Green Book, Colonel Gaddafi's guide to Libya's governance and way of life. Wikipedia offers a rather intelligent definition that puts it into historical and academic context that could be mistaken for a lethal recipe for a very toxic drink. It is described as a mix of Islamic socialism, Arab Nationalism, direct democracy, "the Yugoslav municipal self management of Titoist SFRY and the Yugoslav Third Way as developed by Edvard Kardelj".

At first glance this dispels any thoughts of the book's uniqueness and the claims of many high profile revolutionaries from Gaddafi's old and young guards who labelled the Colonel as a "great thinker" of their time. What you will not find on Wikipedia is the claim by some Libyans that the Green Book was not actually authored by Gaddafi, although one may be inclined to believe that it was. Listen closely when reading the text and you can hear the man's voice. It has that distinct ramble, slightly delusional, and marginally provocative sensation. Is it any wonder that a generation later Gaddafi's heir apparent, Saif Al-Islam, was accused of not authoring his doctorate at the LSE either? Regardless of whether or not the late Colonel authored this three-part manifesto on governance, the economy and society, it came to define the rule of Libya as Gaddafi wanted it to be ruled. It was not the "solution" to the "problem of democracy" or the "Economic problem" as it was proudly labelled on the cover; it was itself THE problem in Libya's governance.

The Green Book's academic tone may seem daunting – and in part it is, although the mildly interesting bits that make you go "hmmm" disappear in to the ether through the sheer amount of ludicrous suggestions in it. I was first introduced to the book by the Libyan embassy in London back in 2004. A diplomat there handed over a copy after many visits to his office to watch a television news channel, and drink coffee with long awkward silences. The reason I kept going there was my feeble – yet eventually successful – attempt to bore the embassy into granting me a work visa.

"So they don't forget my case" I thought to myself as the months went by with no word from the embassy, and so I would arrange another visit.

The Green Book that they handled like the Koran or the Bible at the embassy was proudly handed over with instructions that I should "read and learn about Libya".

The first time you read it – or rather skim through it – you may expect it to appeal to your romanticized image of a "revolutionary". It is embarrassing to admit that's how I approached it. Then I read it a second time – every word, every page – and realised how short-sighted my first impression was. It is, in short, ludicrous. For example:

"It is an undisputed fact that both man and woman are human beings." – Green Book

"A woman, being a female, is naturally subject to monthly bleeding. When a woman does not menstruate, she is pregnant." – Green Book

At the risk of being accused of quoting all this out of context, these revelations and many more besides, were used to illustrate that men and women had equal rights but were unequal in strength.

In short, the book is at times complex in governance, mildly utopian in vision, contradictory by nature and more often than not, simply states the obvious. The "obvious" is especially abundant in the third part of the Green Book, which addresses society.

Below is a summary of the Green Book devised for the curious. It will provide the opening line/s of every theme in the book's three sections or every theme's main points. It may be viewed as "out of context" due to its compressed state, but I can assure you I am quoting it verbatim.

Many of Colonel Gaddafi's theories contained within the book were either implemented with devastating long-term effects on the people or used to create ad hoc state decrees that seemed to experiment with just how far the State could push its citizens. The bottom line is that "the people" were stripped of all power the day it was introduced.

Part 1: The Solution to the Problem of Democracy

The Instrument of Governing is the prime political problem which faces human communities. Parliaments are the backbone of

traditional democracy as it exists today. A parliament is a misrepresentation of the people and parliamentary governments are a misleading solution to the problem of democracy. The Party is the contemporary dictatorship. The class political system is the same as the party, the tribal, or sectarian system. Plebiscites are a fraud against democracy. Those who say "yes" and those who say "no" do not in fact express their will…this is the most cruel and oppressive dictatorial system. Popular congresses are the only means to achieve popular democracy. Any other system of government other than popular congresses is undemocratic. Law is the other problem parallel to the problem of the instrument of governance. It is invalid and undemocratic for a committee of a parliament to be entitled to draft the law for the society. The question that arises is: who preserves the society from any deviation from the law? Society is its own supervisor. If an instrument of governing is dictatorial, as in political systems in the world today, the society's vigilance towards deviation from law will have only one way to gain readjustment. That is violence, which means revolution against the instrument of governing. The natural person has freedom to express himself even if, when he is mad, he behaves irrationally to express his madness.

Part II: The Solution to the Economic Problem

Partners not wage-workers. Wage-workers are a type of slave, however improved their wages may be. The income of any man in the society should not be a wage from any source or a charity from anyone. Man's freedom is lacking if somebody else controls what he needs. No one has the right to build a house, additional to his own, for the purpose of renting it, because the house represents another person's need…in need freedom is latent. A person in need is a slave indeed. Land is no one's property. The legitimate purpose of the individual's economic activity is solely to satisfy his needs. Therefore no individual has the right to carry out economic activity in order to acquire more of that wealth than is necessary to satisfy his needs because the excess amount belongs to other individuals. But the final step is when the new socialist society reaches the stage where profit and money disappear. In that final stage profit will automatically disappear and there will be no need for money. Domestic servants, paid or unpaid, are a type of slave. The house is to be served by its residents.

Part III: The Social Basis of the Third Universal Theory

Nations whose nationalism is destroyed are subject to ruin. There is no other solution but to be in harmony with the natural rule that each nation has one religion. To the individual man the family is of more importance than the state. Societies in which the existence and unity of the family are threatened, in any circumstances, are similar to fields whose plants are in danger of being swept by drought or fire, or of withering away. A tribe is a family which has grown as a result of procreation. Equally a nation is a tribe which has grown through procreation. It is therefore of great importance for human society to maintain the cohesiveness of the family, the tribe, the nation and the world in order to benefit from the advantages, privileges, values and ideals yielded by the solidarity, cohesiveness, unity, intimacy and love of the family, tribe, nation and humanity. Tribalism damages nationalism because tribal allegiance weakens national loyalty and flourishes at its expense. According to a gynaecologist, woman menstruates or suffers from feebleness every month, while man, being a male, does not menstruate and he is not subject to the monthly bleeding.

Reality check:

- Power was centralized in what was the equivalent of parliament but with a longer title – General Secretariat of the General People's Congress
- Ministers – largely composed of the senior members of the Revolutionary Committee Movement – were known as "secretariats"
- In the early years, if anyone on a people's committee dared question the way things were run or, worse still, to criticise Gaddafi, they were hunted down by the state. The forums were mainly used for people to voice their personal problems and when Gaddafi was in the audience he would proudly declare a solution for Mr X on the spot. For example, he would say "you will get a home tomorrow".
- This practice allowed Gaddafi to keep his head above water for decades. He was, at times, like their very own Santa Claus.
- All Libyans working for the state were in fact wage-workers. They were stakeholders in nationalized entities on paper but curiously never really managed to "share the profits" of production because every year, the entity they worked for would declare a "loss".
- All these practices made Libyans heavily dependent on the state.

For more details on the *Jamahiriyah's third way*, I urge you to read a copy – if you can find one. A Libyan friend who returned from Benghazi after Tripoli fell informed me they had a "Green Book burning day" in his hometown. In Tobruk, in the east of the country, a huge concrete replica of the Green Book was one of the first symbols of the regime which the protestors destroyed.

At school, learning the Green Book was mandatory. The lessons were given by something called the Jamihiri Society. Ask a Libyan what they recall from that course and you are likely to get the following answer:

"I remember the part that says: 'the school is served by the students, a child is raised by its mother, the home belongs to its dweller, the home is served by its owners, committees are everywhere (the revolutionary committee movement that is).'"

I wondered how it felt for these children to learn all this. The answer you are most likely to come across is:

"I was confused, I didn't really get it. Now I'm an adult and looking back I know it was an attempt to indoctrinate us... the students did not like it."

In other cases the teacher treated the course like a recreational period. They would allow the students to go out and play instead.

The mandatory Gaddafi course will no longer be force-fed in Libya's schools.

CHAPTER TWO

THROUGH THE LOOKING GLASS

Welfare State

Libya's economic and social policies encapsulated in the Green Book helped transform the nation into one almost entirely dependent on state handouts. There are some people in the country who have been receiving three or four state salaries without having to work a day in their lives. There are those who squatted in other people's properties. That was because it was written in the Green Book, and decreed in a speech by Gaddafi, that "Libyans should not rent" and "every Libyan has a home". Thousands of Libyans lost their hard-won properties in the process with no law allowing them to remedy the situation. It was those who benefitted at the expense of their countrymen who were among the Colonel's staunchest supporters. Now, they stand to lose everything and some are undoubtedly looking ahead nervously as they prepare to face their past.

In the mid 2000s, the Colonel's "reformist" son, Saif Al-Islam, introduced a process to compensate those who had lost their properties. The tone suddenly changed; officials, and at one point Colonel Gaddafi himself, accused Libyans of "misinterpreting" the old decree. So, about three decades after it was imposed, a handful of fortunate Libyans received compensation for their stolen property. Sorting out the mess of who owns what will be one of many challenges for Libya's new governing authority.

In the late 1970s a series of "market-complexes" known as *Souk Al-Moujamah* were created in some of Libya's major cities. They operated in large closed spaces where Libyans could shop for anything they desired. Today these complexes have largely been converted into conventional, privately owned supermarkets. Back then, though, these were state-run facilities where all the goods were subsidized, even Rolex watches. Libyans loved them. One said to me:

> *We found everything there; the best and most recent perfumes, the latest fashion lines from Europe, lingerie, and electronics. It was all dirt cheap; you could get a Rolex for $500 if not cheaper. Back then the local exchange rate was 0.30 kirsh to the dollar (today it is 1.2 LYD to the dollar), so it was all affordable to most Libyans. You cannot imagine what I'm talking about unless you saw it. It was short-lived though; it bred corruption to unimaginable heights. These were state owned entities and the people that ran them pounced on the opportunity to benefit from the process. They would buy some of the stocks that were shipped in, and stash them in warehouses to sell them elsewhere. Many of the clandestine traders were Russians, Czech, Romanians and Bulgarians. They would buy the stocks from them, ship them abroad and sell them in various countries for a sizeable profit.*

It is perhaps inevitable that a state-sponsored gesture that pleased many locals also filled the pockets of officials. The market-complexes lasted till the early 1990s, but were only fully stocked in the first few years because of later corruption.

There were also other subsidized goods given out in bulk on a district-level to every family that presented their "family book" (an official registration booklet for a Libyan family unit).

The local Jamiyat ("organizations") as we call them were the equivalent to state-run supermarkets. Each district had a few trusted people from their areas who ran them and they would regularly meet to decide what was "needed" by people in the neighbourhoods. Then they would go to the state distributor of the subsidized goods, gather their order and bring it back. Families would converge on these. They were seen as more effective because there was little opportunity for corruption in that process. This is where families could get their box of tomato paste, or 50 kgs of Flour and sugar and oil, etc. for a symbolic fee. But everything they bought was recorded in the family book, so the distributors could make sure they were not taking more than they needed.

You would be forgiven for thinking all this sounds rather unnecessarily bureaucratic and primitive – it was.

They were most popular at a time when private businesses were banned by the state. These "organizations" sometimes brought in women and men's lingerie that were distributed as well. They would bring in large bags of undergarments, divide them into small black plastic bags with – for example – a bra and woman's underwear and another bag that has socks and other garments. They were all in random sizes. They would throw the bags out onto the crowd of outstretched arms and then people would exchange their "lucky catch" according to their needs – until they located the right size or type of clothing they required. It was around that time that Gaddafi was also trying to encourage a barter economy so he could cancel money, like he says in his stupid Green Book.

The Great Man-Made River

This was an extraordinary engineering project which Gaddafi described as "The Eighth Wonder of the World". It was a series of pipes that pumped fresh water from deep below the Sahara Desert to the coastal area of Libya where ninety per cent of Libyans live. At nearly 3,000 km it is said to be the largest network of underground pipes and aqueducts in the world.

I am not entirely certain why, but an old copy of the Lonely Planet Guide on North Africa, which included the smallest ever section on Libya, suggested the project may *simply be indicative of a desert Bedouin's high regard for the value of water in an arid land.* It continued, *whatever his reasons, Gaddafi has continued to nurture the project and has protected it from the savage realities of an economic slump.*

Although many believe Gaddafi created the Great Man-Made River simply to immortalize himself, it was, and is, an outstanding feat of civil engineering that fed and continues to feed many cities and towns with water from up to 500 metres beneath the desert.

However, there are many basic misconceptions about the Great Man-Made River Project; first and foremost is that it was the Colonel's vision. This was undoubtedly fuelled by the abundance of posters or billboards that often contained an image of the Colonel, alongside a desert scene of massive concrete pipes which came to symbolise the project. Indeed it was claimed he was its "builder", the visionary behind it all.

The following is the actual history behind the man-made river project, as explained to me by a long-time senior manager of its operations in the eastern part of Libya.

The original name for it was the Coastal Built Water Project. It was a plan derived in the early 1960s (before Colonel Gaddafi came to power) – when the water was uncovered during routine oil drilling in the desert. At first it was thought that it should just be used for agriculture in that area, but in the 1970s a man called Bashir Jouda, the then Minister of Agriculture came up with the idea of transporting the water to the coastal cities for agricultural use – by building dams and that sort of thing.
Kellog Brown & Root, also known as KBR – a US engineering and Construction company developed the concept of this project in the 1980s. When the US sanctions were imposed, operations transferred to the company's British subsidiary and later to its North African one. Other countries in the West like Spain and Germany were also involved in its construction.
Contrary to belief, this project was not solely funded by the state; the government invested LYD 500 million or approximately $413 million only. To date the project has cost LYD 12 billion. The rest of the funding came from a special tax imposed on Libyans, including the tax on tobacco, letters of credit, airline tickets and what was known here as the Jihad tax. That was the money used to construct the project.
Colonel Gaddafi hijacked the entire project; the money was from the Libyan people, the idea was first conceptualized in the early 1960s and it was realized by the Americans and the Brits. Today, after the real Libyan revolution, we are trying to separate his image from the man-made river.

This did not deter officials here from making the Great Man-Made River Project a mandatory part of the itinerary with visiting foreign journalists to waste their time. Others included the impressive ancient ruins sites of either Sabratha or Leptis Magna to the west and east of Tripoli.

Some years ago, I came across a Canadian journalist who had travelled to Tripoli with many others to cover an official visit. When we asked what he'd been doing all day, he groaned, "We went to see the Great Man-Made Boring Project. They just took us to some command and control centre for the pipelines" he continued as he rolled his eyes to the back of his head. "The Great Man-Made Boring" project is how I have referred to it ever since.

A Very Hairy Cultural Revolution

In the 1970s, Muammar Gaddafi announced the launch of his "cultural revolution". In most parts of the country this involved having a bonfire. In the *Maidan Al-Baladiyah*, or City Council's Square in Benghazi, the revolutionary loyalists of Colonel Gaddafi took out all the books from public libraries. They were piled high and set on fire. Similar scenarios were repeated in the capital and elsewhere. Once vital records of who owned what property in Libya were also burnt – that was to enforce his philosophy of "the home belongs to he who dwells in it".

Western music met a similar fate in the early 1980s. There were public bonfires of prized albums, cassettes and musical instruments. It explained why, in later years, many of Tripoli's taxi drivers were so discrete when they slipped a cassette tape into their car radio. It was usually of Pink Floyd, Lionel Richie or – the most modern music anyone seemed to possess – Mariah Carey's first album. It was a daring act, reserved for special occasions – when a foreigner entered their car.

That reality changed quickly as Libya's ties with the West improved. The internet gradually became more widely available around 2005 and the joy of pirated music downloads was discovered. CDs finally replaced the precious cassette tapes smuggled in from abroad, and Libya's shops and markets were filled with the latest Hip Hop, Rap and modern Pop tunes from Eminem to Beyoncé.

These were the sounds that soon blasted from the freshly installed CD players in Libyan taxis and private cars. The tunes later developed into House music and techno. This was not necessarily viewed as a positive development amongst all Libyans. There was something oddly charming about a rich country that was forever suspended amidst the musical lyrics of the 80s and 90s. Other items turned to ash following Gaddafi's cultural revolution included magazines and movies. It is no wonder perhaps that the old, seedy, smoke-filled cinema lined with wooden chairs that survived the test of time in Tripoli's 1st September Street was only showing Rambo II when I visited in 2007. A few years later Libya's first privately owned modern cinema opened its doors in a residential compound along the coast in Western Tripoli's *Janzour* area

The regime's cultural meddling did not stop at the arts, literature and entertainment industry. The state even intervened in people's dress – though mostly for political reasons. Events like the banning of blue jeans became part of Gaddafi's anti-Western rhetoric. Libyans used to call jeans *sirwal Ameriqui* or "American pants". Young people found themselves being pulled over by security officers in public. "Ha!", the officer would say, "you're wearing American pants!"

I am told that some over-enthusiastic loyalists went as far as to strip some young men of their pants in the street. I suspect that Levi's international sales dipped a little in the 80s. Now they know why. Towards the end of that decade, the jean-loving population was safe again.

El-gorwata, which is Libyan slang for the tie was also a contentious issue under Gaddafi's regime. There was time in the late 80s when the tie was banned as well. State television even composed a song against it – *khaneg roha bil gorwata, wa nasee masdarha bee abata* – the lyrics of which many Libyan men recall. It translates to *He is choking himself with a tie, and he has stupidly forgotten its source*. These words alluded to the West as "the source", at least that is how some interpreted it. Others said that it was banned because it looked like the holy cross. Overall, till this day, no one really understands the reasoning behind the short-lived ban. Libyans of Tripoli and other major cities in the country like Benghazi were highly influenced by their Italian colonizers' dress-code; the suit and tie was a staple in Libyan fashion amongst the merchant class. The long-term effect of the ban which seemingly melted away eventually – though few are sure when – is still seen today as many Libyans explain why they are no longer used to wearing a tie.

Libyans also tell me how in the early seventies, when many men still sported the "hippy" look with their afros, Colonel Gaddafi would lecture students in schools and universities and tell them to cut their hair. After he said it the first time, the security services began hassling youngsters who failed to comply. Two years later, Libyans saw Colonel Gaddafi emerge one day – after not seeing him for many months – with his own afro.

His hair gave birth to the now infamous term used to mock him – *shafshoufa* – or "mop-head" as we media hacks would translate it. It is Arabic slang to convey "messy, frizzy hair". This was a widely used term long before the uprising but it thrived throughout the months of conflict to topple his regime. In the past, Libyans would privately mock Gaddafi's unruly locks, saying "look at his *shafshoufa* hair, it's embarrassing, he makes it look like he can't afford a hairdresser".

Mass Health and Education

Once, as I walked my landlady home from the run-down public school she taught in, the inevitable discussion on the state of education in the country arose. I had visited her school for a story I had been working on for the *World Service*. That's where I met an English teacher who asked to be interviewed in Arabic, as she struggled to converse in the language she taught. I met many others like her in the years that followed. There are those who argue that Libya's literacy rate was the highest in the region and that education was free for all. That was true, but literacy on its own was never the problem. The issue was and remains the standards of public education and they were extremely low – arguably the lowest in the region. Almost every public school I came across in Tripoli was in a wretched state, and those farther afield in cities like Tobruk to the east or in Sebha in the south were even worse. Long before the Libyan conflict of 2011, public schools here seemed to carry the scars of a warzone or at the very least, appeared severely neglected.

Part of the problem was this: the regime tried to contrive the illusion of a healthy jobs market, inserting people into roles that didn't exist, or into work they were not properly qualified to carry out. That meant the schools were often run by unqualified "teachers" on extremely low wages. It was the same in many other state-run institutions.

I would often walk into an office and find at least three men sitting idly on a sofa in front of the secretary's desk. They were not visitors; they were employees with nothing to do and no office or desk space to work from, they were just present. Those who were qualified and actually carried out the work were often paid the same wages as those relaxing on the sofa.

Even then, the regime still had a very high unemployment rate – officially set at 13%, though in reality some officials privately said it was much higher and "closer to 25%".

Health, like other state dominated sectors suffered as much as education. Observers would argue that Gaddafi made healthcare free and available to all Libyans. But they missed a key point which gives an insight into the *quality* of that healthcare: most Libyans travelled abroad for treatment. Even those who could not afford to travel would borrow money and make their way across the border to Tunisia for its efficiently organized and "safer" hospitals. Others opted for Jordan, Lebanon or Egypt.

It is not because there was a shortage of Libyan doctors and nurses qualified to do the job. There were many, but often the best fled to work abroad in Canada, America and the UK. The talented ones who remained had little financial incentive to work.

The miserable state of most public hospitals and clinics in Tripoli and elsewhere in Libya also made them highly undesirable destinations for the sick or dying. Patient after-care was a foreign concept here – unless you were a foreigner, in which case they would "take extra special care of you".

Healthcare was in a chaotic state for many years because the government would import the world's leading medical technology, and then wouldn't be able to use it. The equipment would be kept in storage. "We didn't know how to operate it" doctors would explain. Other healthcare facilities were simply rundown and in short supply of everything from medicine to syringes.

I had never seen medics in Libya work as hard or as passionately as they appeared to when the conflict unfolded across the country in 2011. They took many by surprise despite the difficulties they faced – endangering their own lives and often working with scarce supplies. There was a touching moment in Benghazi when the first casualties of the fighting arrived at the main hospital there. The doctors and surgeons applauded them as they were rushed through into the operating theatres.

In Tripoli's hospitals, the scene during the conflict was very different. Security people, mainly from the Revolutionary Committee Movement flooded the corridors and wards to maintain a watchful eye over who was brought in and treated. On February 20th and 25th – when Tripoli's residents took to the streets in large numbers against the regime – doctors said that the injured civilians with bullet wounds were spirited away by the regime's henchmen. Some disappeared; others were given back to their families. Many of the nurses in some of the larger hospitals were staunch regime loyalists aligned to Gaddafi's Revolutionary Committees. When the capital fell into rebel hands, there was a severe shortage of nurses in Tripoli's hospitals the next day.

No Poor People

In a country where there were officially "no poor people" it was often difficult for those with money to help those without. Non-governmental organizations were virtually non-existent under the Gaddafi regime, so too were private charity foundations. The only ones that officially operated in Libya were Aisha Gaddafi's Waatasimo Foundation and Saif Al-Islam's Gaddafi Charity Association. I often met women who told me of their "secret" charity organizations and how they collected money to help others: "We cannot operate openly, only Muammar's daughter can do that." It was a perplexing reality beyond comprehension.

I never understood why the state came to view charities as a threat to national security. If Gaddafi's daughter, one of his sons, and the state no less were allowed to give handouts, then why not let others in the country participate in the process too?

"It's to show that only Gaddafi and his family cared for others and that only they can help the poor – who they even refuse to call 'poor'", a Libyan woman once explained to me. However there were times in the final years of his rule when Gaddafi started making references to the "poor" of Libya – often angrily – as he blamed the government he reigned over for allowing poverty to take a grip. There are some who might argue that not everything can be blamed on the Colonel because so many of those close to him were corrupt opportunists too, and he could not have kept an eye on them all. That may be true, but he created the system that was responsible for the situation, and he was involved in the killings and disappearances of those who opposed that system. It all leads back to him and, in more recent years, to his children as well.

An Expat in Tripoli

Mike is a long-time resident of the capital – Libya was and remains his home. My husband and I visited him for a lunch in the early months of the uprising. It was a brief respite from our claustrophobic existence at the time, when many of our days and nights were spent huddled indoors. It was one of the few times we enjoyed a small gathering that brought together our usual group of friends in the capital – what was left of them anyway. Many of those we knew had fled the country by then. Over a large pot of *Pasta Arabiata*, freshly baked bread and an even larger tray of *Moussaka*, a traditional Greek dish made of aubergines, the conflict and its repercussions on besieged Tripoli was an inescapable topic. We had not seen Mike in months.

Mike was older than the rest of us, and had taken on the role of a father figure. He looked around the room and began warning us of the dangers of social networking sites – even though the internet had long been shut down by the authorities at that point.

"Don't write anything on Facebook or even Skype, have you used Skype? I kept telling my son not to use Skype. They are monitoring everything!"

"I got rid of my Skype account a long time ago" his son chipped in.

"I have lived through this before, you know in the 80s we couldn't even speak in our own homes about the regime or Gaddafi, there were cars parked outside that could listen in to everything you said" Mike added.

Someone closed the kitchen window.

We left before sunset, an unspoken curfew at the time

because the reviled civil guards and other security units often set up checkpoints at night.

Mike remained in Libya throughout the 2011 conflict, although he promptly sent his wife to England at the start of the uprising. As a younger man in the 1970s onwards he was one of the few foreigners who had witnessed the effects of Gaddafi's rule on the country and its people.

We went to see Mike again for another lunch after the fall of Tripoli, along with the same group of friends. His Libyan neighbour was there too this time. It was a starkly different encounter; we were all relaxed that day over the large pot of traditional Libyan *couscous* with enough meat to feed some fifty people. It appeared as though we were feasting in celebration, not only of the recent changes but also of our own survival after the long months of uncertainty. The Internet was back on and we all video Skyped with his other son in the UK. The new Libyan flag draped across the backs of my husband, Mike and another friend as they posed for a quick picture, all of us with wide grins. It was as good a time as any for Mike to reminisce over the past as we sat down in the kitchen later that evening.

> *When Gaddafi came to power*, he said, *money was circulating; he was spending everywhere, building things like the big souks (markets) where the state sold subsidized goods. People were more comfortable during the sanctions; average Libyans had the souks and could buy all their staple products at very low prices. When the country opened up later, officials made a mistake, they moved too quickly (cancelling subsidies), the poor suffered more.*

The colonel at first targeted the rich with his socialist policies (in the 70s and 80s), then he moved on to the middle-class, but the majority – the poor – were still happy in the olden days.
I remember in the late 70s I believe, the currency changed. Some people heard about the change a week before it happened, but the majority didn't know what was coming. At the time LYD 1 was the equivalent of $3 I think. When the Libyan currency changed the old one was devalued to nothing. The Libyans were then only allowed to withdraw LYD 500 a month. It was communism at its best or worst in this case – he wanted everyone to be on the same financial level. Some Libyans committed suicide as a result of this; it was one of the worst times in Libya's modern history. The move created chaos, people went crazy. If their money was in the bank it was safe, but in a cash society where Libyans often hid their money under the mattress, it was a disastrous move.
The 1980s was the most repressive decade in Muammar Gaddafi's rule. Every time we stood in the street, we were wary of who was watching or listening. People did not gather in public in more than threes because it was seen as a threat and the group could be arrested and accused of something. His security even eavesdropped on us in our own homes. We could not say his name – they had their Mazda's and Toyota Crown's parked in residential streets with special listening machines.

• • •

I had heard that story many times before. The first occasion was on a warm evening at the sprawling Saraya café on the corner of Tripoli's Green Square in 2006 (now renamed to

Martyr's Sq.). The café had set up a large projector screen in its outer terrace for the Football World Cup – there was a match on that evening. One of the people I sat with, Youssef, had recently moved back to Libya after spending many years abroad trying unsuccessfully to shake off the shadows of the regime that plagued his mind. He spent the entire coffee encounter speaking of the past.

Soon, a dozen shabbily dressed young Libyan men gathered outside the café huddling behind the low-rise metal fence surrounding it, and straining their necks to get a clear view of the game on the outdoor screen. They were some of the poor Libyans that officially did not exist. Youssef was impressed with the scene.

"That's great, a few years ago, they would have all been arrested and accused of conspiring to overthrow G (code for Gaddafi)" he said.

I laughed, thinking it was a joke. Youssef smiled.

"I'm not joking, we couldn't gather like that before in public" he explained.

CHAPTER THREE

GADDAFI IN A NUTSHELL

Not Quite the Feminist

The world came to know the Colonel in labels. The "Mad Dog of the Middle East" was a popular one, infamously ascribed to the former US president Ronald Reagan. Never mind that Gaddafi was not in the Middle East at all but in North Africa. He was also the "man with the Amazonian guards" the band of female bodyguards who paraded around him on high-profile occasions. I was told by a well-informed friend that he used them because "women were more intuitive and less likely to be distracted by, for example, a good-looking person of the opposite sex".

Some believed it was initially his way of promoting equality between the sexes, introducing women to a traditionally male apparatus. It may well have started out with good intentions, who knows?

Others said they were part of his theatrical displays of grandeur – a more plausible explanation – during his expeditions abroad. The more sinister reasoning - privately relayed in hushed tones – was that they were his modern-day harem.

One well-informed Libyan once told me, rather demurely. "A lot of these women he surrounds himself with were forcefully taken away from their families at a young age, but some willingly went to him. They were trained to protect him but also to please him and those in is his inner-circle...in a sexual way."

Whatever the truth about his female bodyguards, the reality was that many could never return to their families. The stigma that pursued a woman who served in Gaddafi's security apparatus followed them for the rest of their lives. But there was a retirement plan, of sorts. It is said that, when they were no longer of any use, some were married off to officers who lived within the confines of the Colonel's Bab Al-Aziziyah barracks in Tripoli.

Elsewhere, though, far from being paraded around in lipstick and tight-fitting shirts, women were largely removed from mainstream society altogether. Many families, particularly the more well-off, shielded their daughters from the eyes of the regime and some were encouraged to wear the Muslim hijab or veil. The bikini-clad, mini-skirted women of Libya's early 1960s have long-since melted away. Today, they're mostly veiled.

A visitor to Tripoli during the regime would scarcely have seen a woman in the shops or coffee bars around the city centre. A BBC male colleague of mine observed "It's like a single sex country, even if you're invited to someone's home the husband makes you wait outside whilst he clears away all female presence. Only then can you enter. I've been here for two weeks and it's like womankind was never created."

Libyans did try to justify the situation to foreigners, usually along the following lines.

If Muammar (Gaddafi) or his sons or his men saw a woman in public that they liked, they would try to take her at any price. They would send their henchmen who would come to the family home and demand that she be handed over. They could also try and solicit her through a more direct or indirect approach, through the other women that worked for them. What many families sadly did not realise was that if they stood up to them and unequivocally resisted, Gaddafi's henchmen eventually backed down because this was not a matter they wanted advertised on the streets. A woman's honour can ignite a war in a country like Libya. Most families were submissive because they were just afraid of the consequences. Others were happy and honoured that their daughters were chosen by the leader himself because the benefits were good for them too. He ripped families apart with these practices, he ripped our core beliefs into shreds...and then he would stand in public on a religious holiday and lead prayers.

Exacerbating all this was the fact that Libyan women, and men for that matter, were isolated from the rest of the world for many years. They could not join international rights groups which could have helped them to campaign for some basic freedoms. Libyans were on their own, often isolated within a family unit and unable to mix freely with others who might share the same views. I noticed quite early on what a low opinion many in Libya had of themselves. There were those who regarded Libyans, including themselves, as "uncivilized, like him". And by "him", they meant Gaddafi.

Gaddafi Travels

The Colonel did not just "visit" countries in the conventional sense that we are accustomed to witnessing by heads of state. He completely re-defined the term "excess baggage" – to the extent to which I am certain BA would gracefully bow down to my +5kg in excess weight in comparison.

Muammar Gaddafi's outings resembled expeditions that would rival adventurers across the globe – if only in their flamboyance. In Africa, whenever possible, he travelled by road in a caravan followed by a long convoy of armed bodyguards, horses and camels, "because he dislikes planes" a Libyan colleague once said to me. Camels were not restricted to road trips however; when the need arose they would be flown in a military transport carrier too "because he likes camel milk for breakfast". The "Tent" was a crucial travel accessory too – not the conventional kind naturally, but a canvas palace with chandeliers, deep carpets, and finely upholstered furniture. We saw him insist on it in Paris, Rome and New York in recent years – New Yorkers blocked the move however, much to Gaddafi's annoyance.

His armed bodyguards were occasionally problematic too; especially in Africa, where a substantial group of armed men parading through the streets can easily be misunderstood. In some of the more fragile areas, it can be mistaken for an attempted military coup. In 2006, on a trip to attend an Africa-Latin summit in Nigeria, he made the headlines not for the controversial content of his long-winded speech, but for excess guns. Taking along 200 armed personnel is hardly a gesture of confidence in a friendly country's security measures. The standoff at the airport in Abuja between Gaddafi's men and Nigerian security caused a stir – to say the least. No standoff is complete without a tantrum, however, and that is what the Colonel gave people as he stormed off in anger, threatening to "walk" to the city. The then Nigerian president Olesegun Obasanjo intervened and hours later all parties compromised by allowing just 8 pistols to be brought in.

The "Father" of the Nation

Muammar Gaddafi was not and will not be the only dictator who portrayed himself as the father of the nation; Saddam Hussein projected a similar image in Iraq. In the Arab world, a father's role has historically been superior to any other role. He is the provider, the protector, the defender, and the unquestionable authority in a household. Being the father of a family is a position open to abuse. When you are father of a nation, that potential for abuse is of a different order.

His subjects responded in the only way they could. Gradually, over the years, they simply surrendered their independence to their abusive father. As one Libyan put it, "Gaddafi wanted us to become children; he needed the people to depend on him so he would control every aspect of their lives both directly and indirectly."

I heard different versions of that theory over the years but the essence of the argument was always the same. Reflections like that were often followed by cursing or spitting on the ground.

"Baba Muammar" – meaning Father Muammar was a common term used by the children of Libya. Indeed it was an unspoken requirement. The die-hard loyalists of his regime would point out that he is "our father". In the wider scheme of things, the psychology behind projecting that image is arguably not the smartest of moves. Children eventually grow up, and when they do they often rebel against the authoritative figures in their lives.

"Father of African Unity"

The Colonel was arguably more ambitious than Saddam Hussein. He tried and failed to adopt the Arab world in the 1970s and 80s but managed to – in part at least – nurture the African continent. West Africans will argue he helped destroy it. It is no secret that he played a role in Sierra Leone's bloody civil war. Libya was a training ground for some of the Sierra Leonean rebels' top commanders. Muammar Gaddafi's unfettered support for the ex-Liberian president Charles Taylor, who was accused of backing the rebels in Sierra Leone, did not help matters either. Libya's "father" never seemed to have any qualms about his support of rebel groups across the continent; he often flaunted it but also hid it when convenient.

And the rebel cause was not always one that would inflame opinion in the West. In South Africa, the Colonel funded and armed the anti-apartheid movement as it fought against white minority rule. He then bankrolled the election campaign of Nelson Mandela to help him become the country's first black president in 1994. Mandela thanked him by standing up for the Libyan leader against the West. When asked to sever his ties with the Colonel, he said:

"Those who feel irritated by our friendship with President Gaddafi can go jump in the pool."

Mandela then went on to name one of his grandchildren "Gaddafi".

Across Sub-Saharan Africa there was often high regard for the Colonel. He invested in their countries, created jobs, and handed out cash to the poorest – and some might argue the richest as well – on every lavish trip he made to a "brotherly nation". His tours often resembled an African version of the

Rio Carnival – with the added glamour of bank notes raining on the parade. We watched on television as Gaddafi was driven through towns and villages, cheered and followed on foot by some of the continent's poorest people. But the images evoked no admiration back home in Tripoli. Libyans only resented him the more for it, and the rest of Africa for the way it celebrated his presence.

"Look at him" a friend once told me as we watched state television. "It's disgusting and pitiful, if they love him so much, why don't they take him?!"

I once asked an official in Tripoli why Libya's state-owned investment companies built more projects in the rest of Africa than in Libya. It was casual banter over a cup of coffee outside a conference hall as delegates waited to be summoned back inside.

"It's a business; it's more profitable to invest abroad" he answered. "We don't have tourism here and the people (Libyans)…well they don't really understand all these things, they wouldn't appreciate it." I said nothing, but my eyes must have given away that I wasn't altogether comfortable with what he'd just said. He curtly excused himself and went back inside.

It was an extraordinary comment. I would rather have heard the normal excuse: "the sanctions prevented us from doing it". That was the line delivered time and again by officials when asked why a 20 year-old project for renovation or restructuring had not yet seen the light of day. But even under sanctions, Libya was still producing and selling oil. The state had money to invest millions across Africa and Malta and, of course, into the personal bank accounts of Gaddafi and his cronies.

Libya did not just invest more in the rest of Africa than it did at home; it built things which Libyans had been deprived of for decades. There were luxury resorts with golf courses, hotels, and factories. However, many of the foreign projects flopped. It was yet another reason why Libyans grew to resent the regime's dealings with the rest of the continent. Millions of dollars were being squandered, and it was all coming out of their pockets.

As Libyans would often say, "He (Gaddafi) does not want to do anything positive that would allow us to progress."

Gaddafi's new Libya

The sparkling high-rise buildings in Tripoli are new – largely built within the last three years. There are also shopping malls under construction and recreational public parks. Even so, this was – and still is – the most underdeveloped country in North Africa, despite its riches. There are better hotels and parks in some of the continent's poorest nations.

It was as if there was a systematic attempt for decades to keep it that way so the average Libyan – the one who has not travelled abroad or even out of his village – would know no better. When the country's first 5-star hotel, The Corinthia, opened its doors in Tripoli in late 2003, it was obscenely expensive. However, the regime made it appear a pioneering "achievement". It was equipped with a marble-clad reception area, a health spa, a sumptuous restaurant with a bird's-eye view of the capital, and soon the smart cars of government officials could be seen lining up outside.

I recall visiting the hotel myself shortly after arriving in Tripoli. At the time it was the only place a woman could safely get a caffeine fix on her own. There were no cafes in the modern sense of the word until about two years later. The dozen coffee shops that followed were established around 2009 when Libyan entrepreneurs felt safe enough to launch new projects with a minimal risk of their "great leader" waking up one day and ordering all private businesses to shut-down, as he did in the 1980s.

From the moment the hotel opened its doors, the average Libyan was in awe. Young men would hurry into the luxurious reception area, stand at the rail of the stairs that led to the Italian restaurant above, or by the coffee bar, take a picture with an old camera and scurry out with the biggest of smiles. Mobile phone cameras were not widely in use back then. It's a recollection that many find paradoxical, because it was the footage shot on people's phones that first shed light on the Libyan uprising in 2011.

Some years later I found myself having a similar reaction, when Tripoli's first western style cafés began to open up. They tried to mimic the decor of a Starbucks or a Costa (brands which did not exist in Libya), others were uniquely stylized in art deco fashion; you could kid yourself you'd slipped abroad, whilst sipping a cappuccino in their rather plush surroundings. In those days I often got the urge to snap a photo myself, so I could show friends the new café society of Tripoli.

• • •

I have since often wondered whether the Gaddafi regime regretted the modernizing "changes" they encouraged in recent years. What did they talk about as they watched the uprising unfold? Where did they point the fingers of blame, particularly after the entire eastern region had fallen? I have pictured the colonel rebuking his son Mohamed, the head of the Post and Telecommunications sector, like this:

"3G hah? ADSL and Wi-MAX high speed Internet eh? Cheaper mobile phone numbers? YOU FOOL! Look what they did!!!! LOOK!"

Or to his son Saif Al-Islam, the once heir apparent:

"You wanted 'national reconciliation' eh? Where are the prisoners you released now?! (They were among the first to take up arms in the uprising). Where are all my old enemies who you stupidly invited back from abroad? (One of them became a senior member of the National Transitional Council, others joined the protests.) You wanted reforms ah! OPENNESS! You see what happens when you OPEN the doors of the country, the minds of the people?! You DONKEY!" (The donkey remains the most favoured animal used in Arabic to convey stupidity).

I then imagine the Colonel delivering a theatrical slap across the face.

• • •

In 2004 and for many years before that, the mobile phone chip cost 950 LYD or more – the equivalent of 6 months' salary for your average Libyan. Here was one of the world's leading oil producers, with a small population, and yet few could afford a tiny piece of technology that Europe and America, and most of Africa, were taking for granted. With that much wealth Libyans should have all been mobile-phone carrying, cigar-smoking, suit-clad, jet-setting, "too educated for the likes of you snobs!" But they were not. The majority were quite the opposite.

True, there were no beggars seen on the streets, a fact the state would proudly point out when speaking of its "achievements". But that wasn't because they didn't exist. Rather it was due to the fact that most were too proud to wander the streets asking for money despite the astronomical levels of unemployment. So they begged from door to door instead, relying on the community to extend a helping hand. Or, they entered the illicit world of dealing in drugs and alcohol on the not-so-secret black market.

In 2006, another mobile phone service was launched at the "competitive" rate of 150 LYD, which soon brought down the original operator's fee and then prices for both eventually tumbled. This wasn't because the regime had suddenly seized on the notion of a free market and allowing foreign competition. There was no Vodafone or T-Mobile to compete with. The Libyan state-run telecommunications industry was simply competing against itself. It had created another service after discovering the benefits of mass market sales. And, of course, all the profits went to the same place.

Gaddafi the Orator

You did sometimes get the impression that Colonel Gaddafi and the Iranian President Mahmoud Ahmedinejad were competing in their rhetoric. But in the years since Libya had been accepted back into the world community, Muammar Gaddafi had distinctly toned down his anti-Western slurs.

The Colonel did not just *speak* when he addressed the Libyan people or world leaders – he *lectured*. His words were often issued from behind a podium or the comfort of a chair behind a desk. Sometimes, whilst talking, he would wave around a date palm tree leaf wrapped in foil which he used as a makeshift fly swat...even if there were no flies around. Perhaps it was simply part of that "Bedouin" image he liked to portray, if only to appear as a simple man who reached out to the average citizen here.

A Libyan colleague once asked me if I had ever noticed a red handkerchief that was almost always by his side when he issued an address – I had not until my attention was drawn to it.

"It's black magic, he's very superstitious. He uses it to fend off potential death threats and that sort of thing. It's widely known here" she said in a no-nonsense manner.

Populations across the Middle East and Africa widely believe in the existence of sorcery or magic. In Arab cultures it is often associated with spells being cast on men by women who seek their attention. On other occasions the spells are said to be against women, to keep them away from sons or husbands. However, magic also made an appearance in Libyan politics. Some officials believed spells could be used to improve their popularity. And in turn, many Libyans were convinced the regime was using sub-Saharan African sorcerers to cast spells against the entire population.

In the first few months of the conflict, the rebel fighters regularly caught sub-Saharan Africans around the front lines, men they believed to be mercenaries. In fact, most were more likely migrants who'd crossed from neighbouring countries trying to find work. When the rebels searched them, they would often find a pouch or bag filled with odd trinkets and feathers, which they'd then parade in front of the cameras. They persistently said "look what we found on them, this is sorcery!" It may have well been an attempt at sorcery, but perhaps less for fighting, and more for protection.

Then there was the mysterious case of Gaddafi's newly recruited and high profile supporter, Youssef Shakir. He'd been a former opponent of the regime but had turned into a staunch loyalist. For months during the war he spent several hours every day on state television lecturing against the uprising, rebuking and cursing. And by "cursing" I mean in the paranormal, mystical sense rather than the use of foul language – though there was some of that as well. In the early days of the conflict he performed some kind of spell on live television. Everyone was talking about it for months after. Shakir held a long brown feather attached to a *Seb-hha* (a short chain of beads used by Muslims in prayer or when reciting text from the holy Koran) over his desk and chanted something to the affect of a curse on the anti-Gaddafi fighters.

He did not perform the "ritual" again, as far as I am aware, however a *Seb-hha* was always in his grasp when he hosted his shows and he would intermittently swing it towards the camera with a short decree of *El billa feekhom!* (destruction be upon you), *El billa feekhom!, El billa feekhom* when referring to the rebels and Nato. He may or may not have been a Harry Potter fan, I do not know.

Personally, I would have thought the Colonel needed magic to keep his listeners alert for the entirety of his marathon speeches. I attended more than a dozen of them and, if I was with people I trusted, there's a phrase we would whisper: *"ya ard inshaki ow bla-ini.*" This loosely translates as "I wish the earth would crack and swallow me."

But it never did and so a colleague and I would pass the time reading each other's thoughts, exchanging glances, twitching eyebrows, and successfully muffling our laughter in a discreet corner of the venue. Looking back at my behaviour, it was a rather unseemly reaction from a journalist and quite awkward for me to admit to even now.

There were times when we felt like unruly children in a classroom, pupils who really didn't care what the teacher was saying. We cared even less when a long speech was elongated even further by frequent interruptions of applause, or with chanting and ego-boosting poetry recitals for the Colonel from overzealous adorers in the audience.

As a hopeless mathematician, I have pulled together a formula for a standard Muammar Gaddafi Speech inside the country to a local audience. It is open to adjustments.

35 minutes history (at times distorted) (x) + 15 minutes rant against target subject (y) + 3 minutes complimenting target subject (j) + 5 minutes of additional rant against target in case they believed the previous compliments (p) + 2 minutes of outrageously controversial remarks (s) + 5 minutes on the subject he was supposed to be talking about in the first place (z) = guaranteed headline of sorts (V).

For the infamous address to the United Nations in New York, it roughly works out as:

x1.5 + y2 (j-2) + s2 + z = V, variable "p" didn't surface in its normal place. However, the Colonel's dramatic ripping of the UN charter, which he then tossed behind him, was the equivalent of a "p", and so in the end he did manage to stick to his winning formula.

Gaddafi the orator probably bit his tongue the night he threatened the people of Benghazi with his "Moment of truth" speech. He will have realised later that it was ultimately his own words which persuaded the UN to adopt a resolution against his regime on that same night in March 2011.

> *A small problem that has become an international issue. And they are voting on it tonight... As I have said, we are determined. We will track them down, and search for them, alley by alley, road by road, the Libyan people all of them together will be crawling out.*

> *Massive waves of people will be crawling out to rescue the people of Benghazi, who are calling out for help, asking us to rescue them. We should come to their rescue.*

Of course, the "them" he's intent on tracking down are the people of Benghazi who led the uprising against Gaddafi. That night, they amassed in their thousands in a public square to find out what fate awaited them.

> *The moment of truth has come. If you see the cars with loudspeakers, destroy them; destroy their communications points that are spreading lies to you...*
>
> *Just like Franco in Spain, who rolled into Madrid with external support. And they asked how did you manage to liberate Madrid? He said: "There was a fifth column, the people of the city." You are the fifth column within the city. This is the day on which we should liberate the city. We've been looking forward to that day. And tomorrow we will communicate again, and our cause will continue towards the south.*

He did himself no favours when using a fascist leader as an example to follow; he may as well have likened himself to Hitler and Mussolini at that point. What is even more interesting is that the Colonel actually referred to his supporters as the "fifth column" – historically, it described a clandestine force opposed to the state that helped Franco. In the context of Gaddafi's speech however it was a message to his loyalists to attack Benghazi's opposing populace and those elsewhere in the country that had already armed themselves and taken complete control of their towns. Since then Libya's new authorities have referred to Gaddafi loyalists as the "fifth column".

He continued, *With our bare chests and heads we were confronting the dangers, facing the challenge, we did not initiate this violence, they started it. Of course, these words will have an impact on the traitors and infidels. Tonight they will panic and they will collapse.*

That night, the people of Benghazi, and many others across the country let out a joint sigh of relief, as the news spread that the UN had passed a resolution against Libya. It authorised "any means necessary" to protect civilians, short of using ground troops. News organizations and analysts were stunned at the swift speed of the decision. Even so, inside Libya itself, people somehow believed it could have happened more quickly. There were many days my husband and his family would shout at the screen asking "What are they waiting for?! They want us all to die first?!"

What they did not realize is that it was one of the quickest resolutions of its kind to be approved at the UN. It came exactly 33 days after the first protest in Libya, and on the very night Gaddafi made his now notorious address.

It was another speech, however, that is widely seen as the tipping point that galvanized international action against him. He stood against the backdrop of his wrecked home at the Bab Al-Aziziyah compound in Tripoli, defiant as ever, sporting a traditional camel brown flowing robe with a head wrap and a very modern pair of what appeared to be designer sunglasses with transparent lenses. Muammar Gaddafi spoke for more than one hour that night, threatening to punish people with the death penalty. He was addressing those who defied him – the protestors. He then laid out his plan for the people he called the "rats", his opponents. It became widely known as the zenga zenga (alley by alley) speech. It was the night of February 22nd

> *I am calling upon the millions from one end of the deserts to the other and we will march in our millions to purify Libya inch by inch, house by house, room by room, alley by alley, person by person – until the country is clean of the dirt and impurities…millions will march and no one will be able to stop them. Quickly save yourselves before we begin the March. Tonight will be a peaceful march… to save our children and arrest those who harm them… If that doesn't work there will be another march, and you'll know where it comes from… Who are you? It's time to Work, it's time to march! It's time to Triumph. There's no going back! Forward, Forward, Forward! Revolution, Revolution (thumps podium).*

That was a miscalculated address by any stretch of the imagination. He not only appeared crazed, but his words showed many in Libya and politicians abroad, that there truly was "no going back" and that it was time to seriously consider a new strategy. The Libyans who defied him charged "forward" with what was to transform into a full-scale war and the UN came under increasing pressure to intervene on humanitarian grounds; for once in a very long time perhaps, the United Nations appeared to be standing up for the right cause. The Arab League's endorsement of international moves against Gaddafi's regime also made the body seem relevant – arguably for the first time since its inception.

Gaddafi the Narcissist

The former leader was in power for more than four decades and yet in all that time he refused to call himself President; so what was he exactly? "Leader of the Revolution" was the favoured and obligatory term to describe him. He was fond of describing his seizure of power on September 1st in 1969 as a "bloodless military coup". The actual event itself may have been bloodless, but in the decades which followed there was much blood spilt in order to suppress his opponents, both real and imagined.

His ability to mythologize about himself, to rewrite his own history, was quite remarkable. He even managed to claim triumphs over situations or events which he himself had created in the first place. Take the notorious Abu Salim prison, for example, the political jail where Gaddafi dumped his opponents. In 1988 he mounted a bulldozer and broke down one of the prison walls to "free the prisoners". But they were his prisoners in the first place. He was making political capital by hitting out at one of his own creations.

Not only that, the men he was releasing – with great showmanship – were a small group of inmates he had already decided would be pardoned. Libyans distinctly remember the scene as it was broadcast on state television. What the report didn't mention was that the vast majority of prisoners remained locked away, in squalid conditions, without trials, and being routinely tortured. Remarkably, some die-hard Gaddafi loyalists then began describing him as the man who liberated the prisoners.

Interestingly, a similar ploy was used more recently by his son, Saif Al-Islam. In 2006 he began announcing the release of long term inmates at Abu Salim, and managed to win praise as a "reformer" when, of course, it was his own father who was responsible for jailing them in the first place.

In the 1980s, the regime also imposed a travel ban on some of its citizens. Some years on Gaddafi "saved these Libyans" who were on the state's travel ban list for various reasons, including the rich, the potentially famous and those who had siblings or relatives in America. In the Colonel's country, this translates to "potential threat to power or would-be dissident". His "grand" gesture was also broadcast on state TV; he went to the immigration building, stormed into one of the offices and tore some files to pieces, saying "finish, no more of this, no travel ban on anyone". My father in law, a civil servant whose brothers and cousins were studying or living in the United States at the time, had previously been rejected for a posting abroad in Libya's foreign investment company. After Gaddafi's grand gesture, he was suddenly approved for the position.

But as the sycophants lined up to praise Gaddafi senior, largely because they had little choice, he seemed to sincerely believe his own propaganda. In fact, he didn't just believe it, he flaunted it like a Las Vegas showgirl.

In 2009, at an Arab League summit, following a tiff with the Saudi Arabian King Abdullah, the Colonel declared: "I am an international leader, the dean of the Arab rulers, the king of kings of Africa and the imam (leader) of Muslims, and my international status does not allow me to descend to a lower level." The League summit's Qatari hosts at the time were probably not all that impressed by the revelation.

CHAPTER FOUR

MY BENGHAZI

Benghazi will go down in history as the birthplace of the Libyan uprising. However that accomplishment will not erase the years of suffering the city endured under Gaddafi's rule. It was long perceived to be a place where quiet opposition simmered, and for that, the Colonel punished it.

Back in London, when my Libyan "work visa" finally arrived in February 2004 – almost four months after the application was handed over – I was instructed by the Libyan Embassy, officially known as The Libyan People's Bureau, to have my passport translated.

I got the job done at a cavernous, dreary office somewhere near central London. The first member of staff I met was a woman in her late twenties wearing black shoes and a knee-length pencil skirt. She politely asked me to take a seat and proceeded to rummage through the passport.

I filled the gap in the conversation.

"I'm moving to Libya, I'll be reporting for the BBC from there" I said, as though it was commonplace for a 22-year old female reporter to be packing her bags and moving to Tripoli.

Her pen stopped moving. She looked up, astonished.

"I am from Libya" she said… "why are you going there?"

It was an uncomfortable position – being asked in a rather interrogative manner, why I was travelling to her country.

"To report for the BBC" I replied. Maybe she didn't believe I worked for the BBC, or maybe she meant "why Libya?"

It occurred to me this was my first meeting with an average Libyan, and I was quite excited.

"It's so great to meet someone from there! I don't know anyone in the country, do you have family there? Can you give me their contact details…?"

"No" she replied. "I'm sorry".

She shouldn't be sorry, she should be ashamed, I thought. Where was the spirit of Arab hospitality?

Then she said "I am from Benghazi by the way, it's in the east you know. I'm not sure what you think you know about Libya, but life is hard there…I can't give you any of my relatives' numbers because they'll be afraid to talk to you."

Finally it clicked. "Oh you mean because I'm a journalist! Well I don't have to call or see them for work, just for friendly purposes. I'm sure I'll be going to Benghazi at some stage, it would be good to know that I'll have locals to contact, maybe for lunch?"

"I'm really sorry, I can't help. It won't matter why you call or see them, you're a foreign journalist, which will be enough to cause them trouble."

I recall thinking to myself that Libya didn't sound like a promising journalistic destination. She never gave me her name either.

In retrospect, that woman came to represent the many nameless people that on occasion lent their critical voices to the BBC World Service – grateful that they could be heard but not seen. Most days, however, everything they told me was off the record. They just wanted someone to listen.

In the early years of my posting, a foreign journalist could never travel outside the capital without a government minder or a permission slip from the authorities. I travelled to

Benghazi on several occasions, but never without the official convoy that took journalists there for a media "event" – until I married a Libyan that is, many years later.

The events included the unsettling trial of the six Bulgarian medics and a Palestinian Doctor, all accused of intentionally infecting more than 400 children in Benghazi with HIV. It was a controversial case that eventually saw them sentenced to life imprisonment by Libya's Supreme Court. In fact, they were secretly extradited to Bulgaria soon after, with a last minute, rather bizarre, intervention by Nicholas Sarkozy's ex-wife and with the help of Saif Al-Islam Gaddafi. They were pardoned by the Bulgarian president upon arrival in Sofia.

At the time, the families of these children appeared to genuinely believe that the HIV infection was injected into them as part of a conspiracy constructed by Western intelligence agencies. I often wondered if it was only because they were unable to openly blame the state for negligence in the health sector.

On the third or fourth occasion I was in Libya's second largest city for yet another criminal court hearing, I made an excuse to the government minders at the hotel lobby so that I could slip away. I took a taxi to one of a handful of Internet cafés with a recorder and microphone firmly stashed inside my handbag. Internet savvy people – I decided – would be the best ones to tell me the truth about what was going on in Benghazi.

Inside there was one young man – a customer – and another man in his twenties who appeared to run the place. I positioned myself behind an old fashioned PC and tried to ignore the suspicious looks. I peered at the manager from behind the old screen that I was not making use of. A few minutes in I feared he would get the wrong impression; I was of a similar age to him. Then, I mustered the courage to introduce myself to him as a BBC reporter. After an awkward few moments, I asked if I could possibly interview him, just briefly, about life in Benghazi and his Internet café business. I was asked to leave ever so politely.

"We use VPN [satellite] connection for our Internet…your job, it's difficult, God help you…I'm so sorry I can't help."

Heading back to the hotel, I stepped out on to a street in an area close to it for a quick sandwich; I came across a young woman who looked like a student. I immediately introduced myself with the biggest of smiles, and bags of confidence. Surely she would speak, in the name of sisterhood at the very least.

"I can't speak to you if you want to record or take pictures" she warned.

"No, no, it's fine! I just want to know more about people in Benghazi; I don't know anyone here and I'm curious about life for young people your age" I hurriedly explained.

She laughed.

I was ecstatic! Over the moon even; this courageous young woman was prepared to speak to me. I didn't frighten her.

She asked if I was Lebanese – detecting an obvious dialect – and informed me that she watched and loved *Star Academy*.

Star Academy is a reality TV show for young aspiring starlets that believe they can sing, dance and act. European countries ran it for many years. It resembled the short-lived Fame Academy reality show in the UK. Lebanon runs a pan-Arab version of it, a programme seen by many in the Arab world as a show that challenged many taboos in their cultures and traditions.

Libyans, young and old, worshipped the show in the mid 2000s. One of the first nicknames that strangers in Tripoli slapped on me was "star academy" when they heard me speak. It was a slightly nauseating occurrence at first.

"You're a journalist" she said "that's why you don't know anyone here. We don't speak to the foreign media".

Engaging her in conversation proved difficult; I took a few steps away, hoping she would follow my cue and walk. She did not budge. An uneasy look crossed her face. The enthusiasm had evaporated. It was like she'd seen a shadow creep across the wall behind me.

It is a common mistake that reporters make in a dictatorship, focusing on what they need for the story, and forgetting that these people will have to live with the consequences. She was afraid of the secret police, the Revolutionary Committee members, and the local snitch that might trade information about her for paltry favours. These were the real shadows across Libya, not just in Benghazi.

"I have to go home, I'm late" she said before suggesting that perhaps in Tripoli they would talk to me because "they're more open there".

Clearly she had not been to Tripoli, I recall thinking.

Other memorable news "events" attended in Benghazi included:

- The declaration of Muammar Gaddafi – the man who denounced monarchies and presidencies for decades and opted for the elusive title of "guide of the revolution" – as the *King of Kings* in Africa. This followed a "conference" of tribal leaders from across the continent. It was a mass encounter of lavishly dressed and opulently accessorized African tribesmen and tribal leaders under a very big tent; various gifts were presented to Colonel Gaddafi that looked like sacrificial lambs before the new title was bestowed.

- The Libyan-Italian friendship agreement which, for the first time, saw a former colonial master promise to compensate its ex-colony. As the weeks went by it became clear there would be no cash compensation, but rather some lucrative construction deals that would benefit Italy as well.

The origins of Benghazi's fears

In 1960s Benghazi there were liquor stores, "discos", and even casinos with names like The Riviera and The Olympia. There was theatre too. But all if it was wiped out shortly after Colonel Gaddafi came along.

Benghazi today is a city of almost a million people, most of whom have experienced discrimination of one sort or another. The regime imposed what some described as "internal sanctions" on the city for many years, particularly during the 1980s. The reason was simple; almost every opposition group that formed in Gaddafi's era was based either in Benghazi or the eastern city of Derna. This was their punishment.

It is no secret that the eastern part of the country bore much of the brunt of the wrath of Colonel Gaddafi's regime. Some believe he felt "betrayed" by their dissent because it was where he spent many of his years in training when he was in the army in the early 1960s, leading up to the day he launched a coup on September 1st 1969.

In the past, Benghazi was still widely known as the cultural capital of the country. Its natives, however, disagreed with the term. "Benghazi was Libya's second capital" they would explain.

I soon discovered that many of Libya's most talented poets, playwrights, artists, singers, intellectuals and philosophers were from Benghazi. None of their names will be familiar outside the country; the only ones who managed to gain some international recognition were those who fled.

One of those who stayed was Ahmad Fakhroun, a native of Benghazi and renowned music pioneer in the 1980s. The revelation of his work was the way in which he fused East and West, in what was really a forerunner of "world music". I made contact with him in Tripoli, to see if I could write a feature on him. The answer was no. He said he was dismayed at the "system's" handling of the entertainment field and ranted about how there was "nothing in Libya," adding that he was too angry to speak and didn't need trouble. It was – yet again – one of my many journalistic dead ends.

More evidence that Benghazi was a worry for the regime came through the numbers of suspected political and religious opponents who were arrested there. Many were invariably transported to the notorious Abu Salim prison in Tripoli, where inmates were crammed into appalling conditions, sometimes twenty to a cell. As an attempt at some reconciliation with the city, hundreds of prisoners were set free in the years 2005-2010. Most had been incarcerated for "Islamist Extremism". Some of those I spoke to upon their release said they were jihadists who fought in Afghanistan and Iraq but they had given up their old ways. When the Libyan uprising began they were some of the first to the frontline.

Abu Salim prison played a significant role in the start of the 2011 uprising which overthrew Gaddafi. It's become known as the "17th February Revolution". That was the day the young people of Benghazi and elsewhere in Libya had planned to take to the streets. However, the uprising really began spontaneously two days before that. There was a small and daring protest against the imprisonment of a lawyer called Fathi Terbil. He represented the families of hundreds of men who died in a massacre at Abu Salim prison in 1996. The protest began as a small and peaceful affair, but during the day the crowds grew. By nightfall on the first day, the crowds began chanting "Noodi Noodi ya Banghazi" or "Rise-up, rise-up oh Benghazi". It was a chilling moment. I watched it unfold on one of the first videos of the protest that was uploaded onto YouTube. The video-sharing website had been blocked for almost a year by then and Libyans and others only managed to access it via a proxy-server. I was fearful about what would happen to these protesters. At the time, the only conclusion I could draw was that they would immediately be hunted down and killed by the regime. And after that, I thought, the entire affair would be covered up.

Abu Salim Prison

Abu Salim prison held a central role in Libya's recent history. It was where thousands of Gaddafi's opponents were dumped, and where some remained for decades. It was a place of routine torture, where men were jailed indefinitely and many died. It was also a place where men re-appeared after vanishing years before.

Such was the fear of Abu Salim prison that even people walking past would turn the other way, in case they were hauled inside. No one spoke about it openly.

In 1996, it was the scene of the worst massacre of Gaddafi's rule. For more than a decade afterwards, the regime denied anything had happened. But the details slowly began to emerge. There was no clean water, no medicine, only sporadic electricity. Some cells had only a hole in the ceiling for light. Men were kept in their cells for weeks on end. The prisoners began complaining. A group of them took a guard hostage. There were some negotiations, but eventually inmates were dragged into the jail's exercise yard and machine gunned. 1270 of them were killed.

It's said to have taken less than three hours. The man said to have given the orders was Gaddafi's head of internal security, Abdullah Al-Senussi, the second – though some would argue first – most feared man in the country.

At the time, the Libyan regime not only denied the massacre, it even denied having any political inmates or prisoners of conscience held anywhere in the country. The families and relatives of those killed never received the bodies. Many received death certificates more than a decade later. During all that period they remained in limbo, until 2008, when the events of Abu Salim prison were addressed in this statement from the Human Rights arm of a Charity Foundation headed by Saif Al-Islam Gaddafi.

> *Within the context of addressing the issues pertinent to human rights, the Human Rights Society of the Gaddafi International Charity and Development Foundation announces that it learned, through its contacts with competent authorities and its intense efforts in this regard, that the initial report on the preliminary investigations regarding the circumstances of the Abu Salim prison events in 1996, which will determine*

criminal and legal responsibility for the incident, is expected to be announced in the next few days and will be forwarded to the judicial bodies for consideration. It is known that Abu Salim prison is located in Tripoli city and it was at the time of the incident under the supervision of the military police headed by late Colonel Khairy Khaled. Administratively, it was overseen by the Internal Security Organization (ISO) chaired by Brigadier Mohamed Almisrati, while the responsibility for its management was entrusted to the late Amir Msallati.

It is noteworthy that the incident occurred after a group of prisoners seized the keys of the sections held by one of the guards, whom they detained initially, then blinded, before killing him and detaining four guards. This incident led to the intervention by the prison guards and resulted in deaths and casualties on both sides.

Wednesday, 18/06/2008
Human Rights Society
Gaddafi International Charity and
Development Foundation

The most senior figures they referred to in that statement are all dead. In the years that followed, no one was ultimately held accountable for the Abu Salim massacre and the so-called ongoing "investigation" by the Gaddafi Foundation did not provide any closure for the families desperately seeking it.

That statement was also designed to deal with relentless campaigns from organizations like Human Rights Watch and Amnesty International. The families were cynical about Saif's report, because they firmly believed that it was one of the biggest cover-ups in the regime's history. It was also widely known that those who ran institutions, such as prisons, would have had to take orders from higher up the chain to perform summary executions. Therefore, despite the handful of death certificates that were distributed, there were still many unanswered questions.

In December 2009, Human Rights Watch (HRW) – for the first time – was allowed to launch its report on Libya from inside the country. What many missed back then was that Saif Al-Islam Gaddafi's foundation launched its own, almost equally critical report of the state of Human Rights in Libya at the same time.

Saif's report was an attempt to minimize the impact of HRW's findings, by beating them to the punch. But because he had invited them to launch their own report in Tripoli he cunningly managed to win their praise at the same time as undermining them. He had – as we all knew at the time – employed a top class western PR agency that diligently and genially spun his image. It worked from around 2006-2011; after all, no one saw his "transformation" coming!

Things do not always go to plan however and that news conference to launch HRW's report turned out to be like none other we had ever witnessed here at the time. Some former victims of abuse, initially prevented by security forces from leaving Benghazi to travel to the capital and attend the conference, managed to make it there. And in a rare act of defiance they stood up and aired some of the state's dirty laundry. It was a stunning sight. With foreign hacks who had travelled here to cover the conference and HRW in the room no less, security personnel appeared at a loss as to what to do. No one budged.

That is where I met Hussein Al-Madani, a middle-aged man from Benghazi who said he was imprisoned for seven years with his twin brother – without charge – before his release with an apology in 2002. But his brother died in Abu Salim in 1996. His family was only given the death certificate in July 2009. He later told me that they were subjected to harassment and arrest as they mourned over the death testament.

His ageing mother died of a stroke when security forces raided their home a second time, according to Hussein.

Courtyards of Horror

In the 1970s and 80s, Benghazi was generally viewed as a student city – home to the country's best university at the time, Ghar-Younis. But the students who once idolized Colonel Gaddafi, for imbuing the nation with idealism and hope at the height of Arab nationalism, soon changed their minds.

My mother-in-law, a native of Benghazi, recalls the rapturous sentiment of change at the time.

> *Under the Al-Sanussi Monarchy, before Colonel Gaddafi came to power, newly discovered oil and gas was only just beginning to get exported from Libya. The United Nations used to distribute fish oil pills and tuna sandwiches and a glass of milk for every student in schools across the country. There were Jewish and Muslim Libyans living there at the time.*
>
> *I was 18 years old when Colonel Gaddafi came to power; as students, we were thrilled with the change. It was the era of revolutions – Jammal Abdul Nasser in Egypt, and a young officer here in Libya. But I*

remember that my father was upset – he was a trader back then and he was afraid of the change. He was worried that socialism would be brought to Libyan shores just as it had in Egypt. Colonel Gaddafi idolized Abdel-Nasser and was of course overjoyed when the late Egyptian president said Gaddafi reminded him of himself.

Gaddafi quickly changed after the early 1970s. He nationalized foreign and local private companies. He announced to the public: "Go! March over them and take it all" and they did. They came to the offices of private companies and factories in the country, and they took them over. It was his way of implementing his ideas in the Green Book – his "partners not wage workers" clause. Some company owners remained in their workplace and became minimum-wage employees. Can you imagine that? People were crushed and they were silent; this is what many bitterly recall of the past. In Benghazi the government even took all the farmlands; these were private properties. I don't believe they did that in Tripoli as widely as they did in the East; most of the people in the capital kept their farms.

The reference to "Partners, not Wage workers" at first sight would suggest a utopian scenario. One might imagine that the unemployed, uneducated and the poorer section of society actually became partners. The regime certainly made them believe that they were. In reality they became unqualified civil servants of nationalized entities, with a minimum wage.

My mother-in-law continues.

He took everything from us. It was so hard for the men in our family; one day they owned land the next they had none, one day they owned their own businesses and then they found themselves unemployed sitting at home. I had long since stopped listening to his speeches, we hated him.

Though there was a lot of poverty before Gaddafi – and there is just as much poverty now because of his regime – things were organized. We had a constitution, we had laws that people respected. Everything seemed to get worse in the country when he came to power.

I remember a day my mother came home from an outing with other women. She looked ill. When I asked what was wrong she spoke of what they had seen from afar, a public hanging in the church's courtyard.

No one protested because they were too frightened. There were other executions; they would leave the bodies hanging on lamp-posts in the courtyards for days. So many families cried behind closed doors. There was a series of public executions that was aired on our television screens like a soap opera after that. There was one after the other in Benghazi and later in Tripoli.

The Horrors of Benghazi Personified

Huda Ben-Amer, more commonly known in Libya as "The Executioner", is a good case in point. The Libyan woman – who is a native of Benghazi - spent much of her adult life as its de facto governor and was one of the most loathed personalities in the country. She is a figure I had often heard of over the years but had never met.

Huda was an obscure civilian in Benghazi who became one of Colonel Gaddafi's most trusted people. One only has to hear the words "pulled at the legs of…while he hung from the gallows in front of an audience" to get the chills. That is what she was notorious for: the woman who raced to the gallows, in her hometown of Benghazi, and pulled at the legs of Hamed Al-Shuwehdi, a civil aviation engineer who had returned to Libya in 1984 after years abroad as a student. He was sentenced to death at Benghazi's basketball stadium. By pulling all her weight down on his legs, she finished the job off. The brutal moment was caught on video.

"People were shocked" a native of Benghazi once told me. "From then on she became one of the most feared personalities in Gaddafi's regime, his confidant and our eternal governor… every region, every city, every town knows of her."

So what became of her? In 2010, I was encouraged by some contacts to meet a woman in Tripoli who was cracking down on corruption. She was newly appointed as the head of the *Raqaba Al-Idaria* or the state's auditing department. It turned out to be none other than Huda Ben-Amer.

In the end I chose not to meet her. The reason is this: I was scared. Not just of her, but of what I might say if I met her. I wasn't sure I would be able to control myself. Could I simply ignore her past, and treat her as Libya's leading lady against corruption?

First question – I fantasized – *just how problematic is corruption in Libya and what are your latest findings?*

Second question – *Do you find that the people and officials you investigate for allegations of corruption take you more seriously because you are known as "The Executioner"? Or, have you ever threatened those you investigate that you will pull their legs as they hang from the gallows if they don't confess to their crimes…?*

• • •

In a country like Libya under Gaddafi's rule, the knowledge that you are greeting a man or woman with blood on their hands – whilst giving the impression you are an objective observer – is absolute agony. Western heads of state do it every day, of course, and I have often wondered how they sleep at night with their handshakes over a "mutual understanding" or "budding friendship" or "bringing in some dictator from the cold" or above all, over a multi-million dollar contract.

Their actions were hardly perceived in a positive light by those living under Gaddafi's rule. It does not stop at handshakes or a friendly pat on the back. The former British Prime Minister Tony Blair embraced and kissed Gaddafi as they greeted each other in Tripoli in 2004. Then, in 2010 at an Arab League summit in Sirte, the then Italian Prime Minister Silvio Berlusconi kissed the Colonel's hand – hopefully to the embarrassment of everyone in Italy.

• • •

Even at the start of February 2011, when Tunisians had already overthrown President Ben-Ali, and an uprising was underway in Egypt, I didn't think it would spread to Libya. At the time, my husband said to me, "If anything happens here, it will start in Benghazi, you'll see."

He was right.

CHAPTER FIVE

MY TRIPOLI

In the 1960s, Tripoli was a cosmopolitan city and its residents nostalgically remember the days when they had more than a dozen theatres for entertainment, a wide selection of restaurants and cafes, some sixteen daily newspapers, and a variety of international broadsheets. Its healthcare system was hailed as the best in the region. So impressive was the treatment that big personalities are said to have flown in from the Gulf states, choosing Tripoli's hospitals over their own.

The capital was once a bustling city that took pride in its avant-garde approach to life. Busy suit-clad Libyan men and fashionable women would walk the streets of Tripoli or impatiently wait at bus stops as they hurried to meetings. Among them were more traditionally dressed elders, like the women who sported the *farashia* – a large off-white sheet wrapped around them from head to toe and held closely around their faces with only one eye left exposed to peek out onto the world. Tripoli was home to the country's merchant class, the bourgeois of Libya and the Italian, Maltese, Greek and Jewish residents. It was a time of tolerance when its residents proudly compared their city to Athens.

The original settlers of Tripoli used to inhabit the old city, what I imagine was once a magical place with its vast maze of alleyways and a clear footprint of the Ottoman's architectural mystique. Its *souks* and *hammams* remain, but it is an overwhelmingly neglected area of the city these days, with crumbling stone walls, pitted roads and collapsed houses. It is home to some of the city's poorest people and a vast population of illegal immigrants who've travelled here from sub-Saharan Africa. It was neglected many years before the Colonel came to power, but because he ruled Libya for the longest, the fault for its dilapidated state – as far as Libyans see it – lies squarely on his shoulders.

After the 1969 *Al-Fateh* military coup (an event which only Gaddafi and his officers described as a "revolution"), the transformation of Tripoli was only a few short years away. From 1975 onwards, the Libyan capital witnessed "waves of Bedouins arriving and taking over" as many residents put it. That period is popularly known as the "Bedouinisation" of Tripoli. They came in from rural areas and from the desert and they refused to change their ways to suit the urban lifestyle of the capital. Instead, Gaddafi's regime systematically set out to encourage the Bedouin culture taking hold in Tripoli. A typical view on this matter by the city's older residents included:

> *There was the adoption of the tent and the adoption of the Bedouin culture and customs in Tripoli. In the past, for example, we never had public weddings where we closed an entire street for three days with an oversized tent. We never had that here in Tripoli!*

What they did have, however, was a very organized public transport system. The large buses soon disappeared after Gaddafi came to power, to be replaced many years later by the *Iveco* micro-buses with unruly drivers who simply stopped wherever a passenger stood to be picked up or wherever they wanted to be dropped off along main roads. In some ways perhaps that was more convenient, but it also meant no one really knew what time they'd arrive at their destination.

Tripoli's younger generations, those growing up in the 80s and 90s, were strongly influenced by the Bedouinisation of the city. The older generation was forced to adapt as well. But among the natives of Tripoli, there remained a distaste for what had been imposed upon them, and many would describe the Bedouin characteristics they'd adopted as "ignorant". I had never before heard people describe *themselves* as backward or ignorant or uncivilized, but many a person I met in Tripoli did – even the most educated of them.

It is not that Libya's city dwellers looked down on the Bedouin culture; it is seen as a traditional heritage of all Libyans who trace their roots back to tribes. However, for many in the big cities, that tradition was largely a romanticised notion of vague Bedouin qualities such as "courage and generosity". What Gaddafi managed to do was politicise the Bedouins and the tribes, to create a new class in Tripoli and other major cities across Libya, a class with unquestioning allegiance to his rule.

Other changes came about just as swiftly.

"There was a climate of free speech and freedom of thought" before Gaddafi came to power, Khalifa Shakreen, a Libyan political science professor in Tripoli recalls. He was one of the many expelled from the University of Tripoli, later renamed Al Fateh University, when he was a student in the mid-1970s.

> *Up until 1976, the university was a forum for diverse national groups expressing themselves; it was a national student movement in control of the university and then Gaddafi decided to put an end to all that and we were expelled. After that the university became a platform for*

> *Gaddafi's personality cult and a forum for him to express his ideas to the people through the university. It ended up being a non-learning institution.*

Tripolitarians did not see the tsunami of change coming. They, like many others across Libya, had initially welcomed Gaddafi's seizure of power.

Another Libyan intellectual, Sami Khashkusha, reflected on the sweeping change that befell his city when the Colonel came to power.

> *Gaddafi looked at the Tripolitarians as anti-revolutionaries, as being Italianized and as the remnants of colonialism. He had to replace them. The cosmopolitan culture that existed posed a threat to his new ideas and this culminated in his declaration of a "cultural revolution" in 1973 in his now infamous speech from the western city of Zuwara. That declaration was what changed the course of Libyan history; that was when he ultimately appeared to declare himself a dictator, he declared a totalitarian regime from that day – he suspended all the laws, he declared a revolution against bureaucracy, he declared a revolution against literature, art, music and everything.*
>
> *The public hangings of dissidents started in Benghazi in 1977. In Tripoli, one of the first to be publically hanged was Rasheed Kaabar. It was April 1984, he was a student of pharmacology and was executed at the university after they took him out of prison.*

Then he talks of Outhman Zerti, a man whose hanging didn't go to plan. He survived the initial drop and was swinging and struggling with the rope around his neck. To finish the job, a Gaddafi hardliner ran across and pulled on his legs.

> *I was not in Tripoli at the time but I saw it on TV. Then they put him in a rubbish truck and drove around with his body. Their final destination was the centre of Souk Al-Joumha, next to the police station and municipality of the district; they threw him out of the truck and started chanting pro-Gaddafi slogans and jumped around. Fortunately, the Gaddafi regime documented these scenes which we can see today.*

That was not the only case of its kind in the capital. Many public executions of students, professors or professionals – who were involved in underground political movements or suspected of being dissidents – were staged in Tripoli and elsewhere in the country. Often they were filmed, possibly as a warning to others, but also to flaunt the unbridled power of the regime.

The colonel would even order killings to take place abroad. In the 1980s he called on Libyans who were going to the Hajj (Islam's holy pilgrimage in Mecca) "to take responsibility for fighting and liquidating the enemy and stray dogs if they are found there…". On another occasion he said "It is the Libyan people's responsibility to liquidate the scum distorting Libya's image abroad."

From Beirut to Bonn, London to Rome, and even in the US, Gaddafi's opponents were not safe. At least two dozen prominent and outspoken dissidents of his rule were hunted down and assassinated during the Colonel's "liquidation" campaign in the 80s and 90s. This is believed to have been carried out by a network of Libyan diplomats implanted in embassies abroad, as well as other hired assassins. It is also what ultimately led to the fatal shooting of the British Policewoman PC Yvonne Fletcher outside the Libyan embassy in London.

Libyan dissidents were holding an anti-Gaddafi protest when a machine gun opened fire from the first floor of the embassy. In all, eleven of them were hit. It was a day which re-defined Libyan-British ties for many years.

The now fallen and late Libyan leader also came to re-define the relationship between his people, as one native of the capital put it,

> *After Gaddafi came, he brought his people – the people he trusted, who were Bedouins. They pushed us out. Natives or residents here at that time couldn't work with them anymore – just imagine your boss being narrow-minded, uneducated, not knowing what to do and you have to work under him…how long are you going to do it for?*

The term Bedouin was one I often came across when speaking to long-time residents of the capital. It was one of the most common references made when they would try to explain to a foreigner what befell their city or what changed the mentalities of the people of urban Libya. Many of those who secretly resented the regime in Tripoli would only smile when speaking of the past, the pre-Gaddafi era.

Tripoli of Business

Tripoli was not only the capital, but also the country's financial – thus corruption – hub during the Gaddafi era, although many would argue corruption was rife under the monarchy as well. By the mid-2000s, the city was largely viewed as the "chosen one" for most foreign investment projects in the construction sector. Tripoli also had its run-down neighbourhoods, under-developed infrastructure, and several levels of poverty. However, in the larger scheme of state affairs, Tripoli – and arguably Gaddafi's hometown of Sirte – was always taken care of first. There were Libyans who were of the unshaken conviction that those two cities received the lion's share of state investment. The real question that many from outside Tripoli at times overlooked was who were the beneficiaries of this. The answer was almost always Gaddafi's supporters – the class he created in Tripoli or the wealthy businessmen who worked closely with the late Libyan leader's inner circle.

Development-wise, the situation was not unique to Libya – the capital is almost always more developed than other parts of a nation. I found Tunisians complaining about the same issue under Ben Ali's rule. In Gaddafi's Libya, every big and miniscule fault in the country would come to be blamed on him or his regime. In a place so wealthy there were few excuses to hide behind. Libya had a measly six and a half million people by 2011 and only three million when Gaddafi came to power. With vast oil and gas reserves, and a regime that assumed responsibility for taking care of every living organism and non-living object, it could only be the regime's fault.

Salah El-Aabar, a friendly, soft-spoken professional in IT, is a native of Benghazi who resides in Tripoli. He, like many others once moved to the capital for work opportunities.

> *Gaddafi's power was centralized in Tripoli that's why everyone wanted to come to the capital, all the business was in Tripoli…there was a time when Benghazi's natives referred to Tripoli as Tarablous Al-shakika or Brotherly Tripoli, under Gaddafi's rule.* (a term often used between Arab and Africa states) *It was as though it was a different country, just as Libyans call Tunisia,*

Tunis Al-Shakika. Gaddafi brought his people to Tripoli from all over the country and installed them in superior posts that wielded power.

All these factors combined are what led to Tripoli becoming home to a diverse population of Libyans. As the largest and most populated city in the country, it is also what arguably stalled the "liberation of Tripoli" for seven long months during the uprising.

The Writings on a Page

Tripoli-born Guima Bukleb, a former prisoner of conscience under Gaddafi's regime, was a young aspiring writer when he was incarcerated.

There were sixteen of us and during that time Gaddafi launched his Revolutionary Committee Movement and they started to operate on the political stage and started to look for "enemies" to make heroes of themselves. We were creative writers who wrote short stories for literary periodicals – talking about cinema, and the theatre etc. To them [Gaddafi's henchmen], it appeared as though we were living in a different country from theirs. They started monitoring us and our meetings and because we all wrote and talked about women, life and things like that, they decided we were not just reactionaries and classified us as Marxists…we weren't Marxists; we were leftists, yes, but there was no secret or underground party…we perhaps immaturely admired Marxist theories, but that was it… we were attending a cultural event in Benghazi when we were publically arrested, and beaten on the 26th of December 1978 before being taken to prison.

Guima Bukleb is currently serving as the new cultural attaché at the Libyan embassy in London. I met him during his short visit to Tripoli, some weeks after the country was declared "liberated" by its new authorities, following the death of the Colonel.

"I'm sorry" I said to Guima as he finished recounting his experience.

"Me too" he replied.

"Perhaps now you can write your short stories again," I added.

He wholeheartedly laughed, telling me "we are writing novels now...now we have the time and the freedom."

Arrival in Tripoli

My first proper encounter with a Libyan in Tripoli was with a very friendly, well-spoken senior immigration officer at Tripoli's international airport. His English was impeccable, a necessity at the time because my Arabic was too Lebanese and his was too Libyan. I was ushered into a tiny room at immigration, where about half a dozen officers were frantically trying to photocopy my passport. They had no idea how to process "al sahafiyah!" – the journalist – as they kept shouting across the shabby, depressingly pale interior of the airport. The dilemma was complicated further because there was no government minder to escort me into town – a pre-requisite for a journalist entering Libya at the time.

A Dutch pilot who had arrived on the same flight waited patiently a few metres away to make sure I was okay. We had spoken briefly at the airport in Malta as we transferred planes. He thought it was crazy for a journalist to come here at all. In fact he appeared more frightened for me than I was at the time. Looking back, I don't think I felt much, only confusion.

The senior officer frowned, asked how old I was (he seemed to think I was too young to travel alone, but I was 22 years and 8 months) and then inquired why official minders were not there to meet me.

"I don't know." I answered flatly.

"Did you give them the correct flight details?" he said.

When he'd reported the situation to the press authorities, and established the fact that there would be no official minders coming to meet me, his mood changed.

"I'm so sorry, what will you do now? Don't take a taxi, it's late."

Does he mean dangerous? I wondered. Is he suggesting I sleep in this soviet-style building, with its grubby walls and fog of cigarette smoke and its strange posters which carry slogans like "partners not wage workers".

"It's fine, I have a very good, old friend of mine here" I said as I pointed to the Dutch pilot I met about two hours earlier. He looked about fifteen years older than me, and it seemed obvious we didn't really know each other, but I persisted. "His company driver will drop me on the way, they have a mini-bus!"

"Normally I should not let you into Tripoli alone like this, but it's not your fault so OK, go…good luck" he smiled. I've never had such a pleasant encounter with an immigration officer in Libya since.

The first hotel I stayed in, *Winzrik*, now lies in ruins after a Nato airstrike. It seems they were suspicious it was being used as a command and control centre in Tripoli. We have since discovered an underground shooting range beneath the

Winzrik and a very old media studio – think 1970s – that is almost unused. No one is entirely certain why they are there.

The hotel receptionist – probably not a day older than twenty – made no secret of his "secret agentness".

The night after I arrived, at around 1:40am the room's phone rang: "Hello Madame, it is reception here. Where did you go today, who did you meet?" he stupidly asked. This was also the night after I found my luggage opened and thoroughly searched by "someone" as I had a quick dinner at the hotel's closed restaurant following my arrival. The Moroccan waiter was an absolute star! The spaghetti bolognaise was not.

I put the phone down. It rang again within seconds.

"Hello, do not close the line, tell me where you went today" silence ensued and another demanding "just tell me" followed. It was like a really bad episode of a spy saga.

I played the indignant Arab whose religion had been offended.

"How dare you call a woman at this hour of the night?! Shame on you, may Allah forgive you. Don't call again!" Click.

The phone rang a third time, I did not answer. He appeared to give up on the fifth failed attempt. I did not sleep that night.

The friendly Moroccan waiter lent a very sympathetic ear at breakfast. We communicated in French to ensure that anyone listening would be miserably confused. I could tell from the start he was someone on my side.

"I'm so sorry about this," he said, "you know who the local staff here work for, right?" I nodded. "Why did you come to Libya? It's not good for you here. You are so young, go and report from Morocco, it's nicer there for foreigners. How old are you?"

I felt a sudden urge to pack my things and fly to London. That was followed by a quick reality check. If they had to ask where I was then clearly they were not very good at their jobs. Many months later, as my understanding of Libya matured, I came to understand that those junior informants were in fact terrible. They were not the "real spies" in Tripoli. They were the intelligence gatherers in training, the unqualified men and women told to "keep an eye" on the foreigners and "find out as much as you can about them" in return for a below-minimum wage. It turned out that these people were the least of my worries.

Landlords of Tripoli

My first landlord was in the upper middle-class suburb of Hay Al-Andalous district. I rented the equivalent of a studio on the rooftop of a large family home, with the instruction that men could not visit unless they were accompanied by their spouse or "some woman partner". In addition, all visitors could only be foreigners. "No Libyans allowed, no man no woman" my very Libyan landlord told me.

The ground rules were not bothersome at the time; I had no friends in Tripoli and appeared unlikely to make any for some time to come, even within the expat community. Libya 2004 was not a time when many were prepared to be associated with the first foreign correspondent of a Western media organization in the country. It was perfectly understandable; I would not have associated with myself either given the circumstances.

The "No Libyans" rule was troubling and odd. The landlord's wife, a pharmacist by education and an outspoken mother of three with a short temper, explained it in no uncertain terms months later. This was after asking "do you really only work for the BBC or also for MI6?"

"Are you serious?" I said, "Of course I only work for the BBC!"

"OK, but if you work for MI6 I don't mind" she laughed. "Maybe you can tell them how things are for Libyans here." It was a time of "thawing" relationships between the UK and Libya and some appeared hopeful they would be "saved" by the West after decades of tyranny and long years of international sanctions.

"Let me explain" she continued, "we live in a difficult society…mentalities are 'backward' as they say". She was a woman who seemingly never left her home and appeared to have no friends or relatives in the city to visit or receive.

"You know, even one of my husband's sisters cannot come over, she has friends who are close to the regime…that sort of thing, and everyone is angry with her. You can't trust anyone you meet because you don't know who their friends are or how they think. Gaddafi dismantled family units, he made us behave like this. You know what I mean?"

No I did not, but came to understand her long after I moved out – when her husband woke up one day almost two years later and demanded double the rent for a place that deserved about 60% of what was already being paid. When I protested, he said "there are other foreigners prepared to pay more." It seemed that Gaddafi's distorted socialist principles had created so much uncertainty there was a "grab it whilst you can" attitude.

Libyans had long stopped renting accommodation to their fellow countrymen. Since Gaddafi's decree (mentioned in

Chapter 1) stating that "Libyans should not rent" and that "every Libyan has a home", landlords were afraid that tenants would simply decide to stay indefinitely and for free. This was especially problematic in Tripoli because many Libyans would often move to the capital for work opportunities. The gradual trickle of foreigners as the country "opened up" again provided the perfect opportunity for them to capitalize on their emerging rent options.

This was, in my judgement at the time, a typical middle-class Tripoli family: conservative, paranoid and with a sharp eye for making money.

My second adventure with a landlord in Tripoli could not have been more different. This was a two-income family, with two teenagers. It was an experience that, when relayed to other Libyans, I was told represented the true Libyan spirit "before Gaddafi destroyed us". Najat and Jamal had lived in Tripoli throughout their lives but one was from Tarhouna and the other from Misrata – Libya's third largest city in the west. Almost a year after I moved out we were still in touch, and at the start of the uprising there was an event which illustrated just how much they cared for the foreign journalist who so many others would have been too afraid to help.

Najat called me one night in a frantic mood.

"Rana, are you OK? Are you here? Are you at home?"

Her panic was contagious. What had happened? What had she heard? Had the security services been hunting for me?

"I'm fine, what's wrong?" This was a time we couldn't speak freely over the phone. Instead we had to use code because, if the line was being monitored, anything deemed negative towards the state could result in detention.

"Aaaah...no nothing...are you sure you are at home?"

I was uncertain how to react. In the back of my mind I was afraid she was being coerced by the security forces to find out my movements. I had visited Najat and Jamal about a month earlier and they were some of the few people in Tripoli who knew I was still working, under an assumed name, for the BBC. I had even used some of the information they passed to me in my Tripoli Witness articles. This call could have meant trouble for her, for myself and for my husband and his family.

"Yes, I'm at my place in Airport Road." I lied. I had long since moved to my in-laws by then, in a quiet suburb at the other side of the city.

"So you were not on the state TV channel?" she persisted. I was utterly confused by the question and at one point I began wondering whether, actually, I might have been on state TV. A combination of paranoia and fear can play terrible tricks on the mind, particularly in a dictatorship engaged in a war against its own people.

"I'm fine Najat, I swear… are you ok?"

"Ok good, I thought I saw you on television…someone said they saw you. It's nothing, forget it." she laughed nervously. The conversation soon came to an end but I was left with a lingering fear about the real motive behind the call.

Later that night, all was explained. A Syrian born local journalist, also called Rana, had been paraded on state TV that night and cross-examined about her reporting by an off-camera voice. It was a chilling confrontation, with the journalist berated and sneered at. The voice was easily identifiable as that of the much reviled Hala Al-Misrati. She was the woman who eventually waved a gun live on air before Tripoli fell and vowed she would kill or be killed before she left the station.

Rana – the Syrian journalist – had grown up in Libya and written for a local paper. On state TV she was accused of "lying about the state of affairs in Tripoli" in a conversation during an international phone call. She remained admirably composed though clearly fearful as she answered questions like "You said there is no bread…that all the shops are closed…Why? Are you going hungry? Huh?"

My former landlady, Najat, never saw the broadcast herself, I later found out. It was a relative of hers who called to say, "remember your former tenant, Rana, the journalist who is from Syria or Lebanon that you used to tell us about…?" You can imagine how the rest of the conversation went and how the confusion occurred.

• • •

Najat was and remains a public school teacher and together with her husband, chief of cabin crew for a state-run airline, and two children, they represented the average struggling family in Tripoli. They only just made enough to make ends meet and were disillusioned and embittered by the regime. Nevertheless, they were always cheerful and generous to me, and to anyone else they met. It was a mutual friend who had originally led me to their place in a narrow side-street that was once called The American Street.

The side-street parallel to us was riddled with pot-holes and almost always blocked with residents trying to drive out as they passed a very crowded car mechanic's garage. Urban planning was as disorderly as the regime's Third Way of governance.

In the spring and summer, our street transformed into the most colourful and beautiful in the area with scented flowers spilling over the fences and creating a colourful contrast to the compulsory green paint which characterised the Gaddafi era.

The wooden door to our building was the only one with a timeless rusty metal slot with "Letters" engraved in it. It is a shame it was never used. The only post you ever received in the mid-2000s was from disgruntled delivery boys of a courier service when addresses were described as "after roundabout X, take the second street on your right and drive along until just over half-way down, look out for the cream-coloured wall and copper metal gate…OK you know what just call when you get to the roundabout, I'll pick it up from there!"

Once, out of the blue, Najat marched upstairs to my small roof top apartment. She was clutching a pile of broadsheet newspapers.

"I got these from my mothers home…remember when I told you we have the old newspapers that showed what Gaddafi did to the people who were openly opposed to him? Here they are, look!"

Leafing through the paper from the 80s, the pages were filled with pictures of men and their lifeless bodies sprawled on the ground with text branding them as Islamists.

These were the faces of men hunted down by the regime and paraded on state media. It was not only shown in print at the time, but also on television. Between the 1970s and late 90s Libyans only had access to state channels transmitted from their rooftop antennas; this included state TV and a couple of Italian channels "if the weather was right" they would explain.

"On television they would show the opponents they killed; their legs hanging out of rubbish vans that were driven around the streets of Tripoli. They did it to terrorize everyone else" Najat would say.

• • •

At the start of the 2011 Libyan revolt, the regime immediately branded the protestors "terrorist gangs", much like Tunisia's Ben Ali accused protestors in the tiny village of Sidi Bouzid and beyond of being "Islamists". Islamism and Al-Qaeda are the 21st century's panic buttons for dictators needing urgent support from the West. That is, perhaps, why the French were silent about Tunisia's popular uprising until the very end and why American and British officials re-established ties with Gaddafi's regime around 2003.

The former Tunisian leader soon conceded to the popular uprising, abandoning the charge of "Islamism" with his regionally infamous remark "*Fahimtokom, Ani Fahimtokom*" – I understand you, I understand you" before fleeing the country. Libyans, on the other hand, were met with their leader shouting "*Man antom? Man antom?!* – who are you?!", followed by accusations that they were all high on hallucinogenic pills. The protestors set out to show Gaddafi exactly "who" they were soon after.

• • •

There were countless other times when my landlady would rush upstairs to relay something which angered her about the regime. She was also, like many women here, a very good cook.

The plates of food or sweet treats that were frequently delivered to my doorstep by her or her 18 year-old daughter were part of a very satisfying experience for me.

On my first week as her tenant, Najat delivered two homemade flavoured sugar syrups in glass jars with neatly cut red fabric tied over the lid and topped with a golden ribbon and a small trinket.

"These are lovely! And absolutely delicious!" I said of the orange peel and cinnamon syrup and another made from the leaves of a locally popular aromatic plant called Outur.

"Thank you" she beamed.

"You should open a shop and sell them!"

"Really? You think it's possible? I have always wanted to do something like that…but you know how it was here before… and now everything is just too expensive if I want to rent a shop" she reflected.

CHAPTER SIX

REGIONS, TRIBES AND ETHNICITY

Though Libya was once regionally divided between Tripolitania, Cyrenaica, and the Fezzan and had a federal government for many years until it was scrapped during the reign of King Idriss, the regions did not divide the people. Libya is known as a country of cities: Tripoli, Benghazi, Derna, Misrata, Geriyan, and Zawia are the biggest, and are home to the largest clusters of population. Their residents, though, come from different tribes across the country. A classic example is how most of the tribes in the eastern city of Benghazi actually consist of people from the other side of the country, from Geriyan in the western mountains, and from the western port of Misrata, among others. That is why it is common to meet Libyans whose family names are derived from their ancestral Libyan city, like "Geriyani", or "Misrati". They were names adopted by those who moved to those cities and settled there. However, it did not necessarily carry with it any association with where their forefathers originally came from. Try arguing with my husband, a *Geriyani* – who is from Benghazi – about where he's originally from and you will see my point. The staunch reply is, "I'm from Benghazi."

Libya is tribally-based historically; however, the varied allegiances of the population were not divisive during post-colonial rule in 1951. It is an issue shaped by several – perhaps overlooked – factors in modern times as Western analysts mull over "tribal rivalries" in post-conflict Libya and speculate how that may influence its future stability. There are not many inside Libya itself who believe that tribal differences will have any significance in the future, despite Gaddafi's relentless propaganda in the dying days of his regime. The issues are best summed up by one Libyan man's explanation to me.

> *King Idriss, when he ruled Libya he came from no tribe, he was not even Libyan! He was Algerian, and yet he received the confidence of all the Libyan tribes and cities because he was a knowledgeable and religious man and he wanted to make good for the country.*

In fact, King Idriss *was* born in Libya, in the Eastern desert oasis of Jaghbub – but in Arab cultures, there is a tendency to define one's nationality through the male ancestral line. The King's great-grandfather's roots apparently lay in Algeria.

Some also argued that the King was brought to power with the help of Western governments. However, King Idriss came from a long line of prominent religious scholars who roamed the region with a large following known as the Al-Sanussi Order – who traced their lineage back to one of the daughters of the Prophet Mohamed. Before reigning over Libya, King Idriss was – at first – the Emir of Cyrenaica (the east) and later of Tripolitania (the west) but it is the eastern region of Libya that was ultimately his stronghold until the Federal Kingdom was formed. Historically it was fighters from the east who joined him in warfare against the Germans and Italians during World War II.

It is said that in 1977 Gaddafi was receiving delegations from different tribes in Libya who pledged allegiance to him and were made to sign documents to that affect – apparently in blood. This, it is believed, was the turning point in Libya's social history. Contrary to many views, Gaddafi largely encouraged tribalism so that he could control it – and he did that by the age old tactic of divide and conquer. In different periods of time, Gaddafi would empower some tribes over others. The objective was to perpetuate his power rather than the common misconception that he controlled tribal rivalry by uniting them.

However, even decades into Muammar Gaddafi's rule, I rarely came across Libyans who spoke on behalf of tribes. Some of the issues we hear about today were, undoubtedly, introduced during the nine-month conflict. People today are quick to claim the tribe they belong to and their city of origin. This is largely seen by Libyans as a natural post-conflict reaction because of the battles fought in almost every city or town and Gaddafi's seemingly desperate attempt to create divisions as he clung to power in his final months. Scholars and observers in the country believe that will soon fade away because it is not ultimately an issue that is historically ingrained in Libya's society or politics.

Tribalism is part of the social fabric of Libya but the country is largely considered a homogenous society. Under the Kingdom, the officials in parliament were from across the country and Gaddafi continued the trend, but that does not mean it was built on tribalism – the tribes were never involved in the day-to-day decision making of the country and in the last few decades they only ever played a minor role on a social level, like intervening in family disputes.

One could argue, though, that in a time when history is being re-written after such profound change, anything is possible, however unlikely it might seem right now.

The most recent developments in post-conflict Libya can be seen as a promising sign of the political direction the country is taking, despite the many unknowns that lie ahead as Libyans clean up the debris of a war that inevitably left behind the footprints of forty-two years of dictatorship.

A Libyan said to me.

Look at our new transitional prime minster today. He is from Surman (a western town in Libya). He lived all of his life in Tripoli – go and ask anyone in town, everyone knows him – he was playing basketball in Nadee Shabab al Arabi (the Arab Youth -Club) and many people went to school with him. Nobody knows he's from Surman and they couldn't care less!

Another said, *Even as Gaddafi fell, none of the tribes stood by him to defend him – not even in his hometown of Sirte – it was all propaganda.*

It was Gaddafi's trained forces or hired mercenaries who fought for him in his dying days in Sirte. Civilians who supported him ideologically simply fled, including members of his tribe.

Though Libya is ethnically diverse with its Arabs, Amazigh, Tuaregs and the Tabu, Libyans do not believe it was ever a political or social issue. That is, aside from the regional and ethnic stereotypes that people categorized each other in and at times the glaring racial divides as some whiter Libyans looked down on browner Libyans who looked down further on black Libyans.

In the 1970s Gaddafi tried and partly succeeded in selling the pan-Arabism outlook. The country's "Arabists" began to rewrite the history of Libya, eliminating the parts that were not beneficial to the regime. Minority ethnic groups in the country saw the state's move as an infliction of social injustices against their identity. It is believed by many Libyans that this is what caused some minorities in the country to become even more conscious of their identity. This was even followed by the imprisonment of some Libyans when they publically expressed a cultural affiliation – it propagated further resentment against the regime until the day it was toppled.

As a reporter, I did not easily have access to Libya's minority ethnic groups, particularly those from the South, the Tuaregs and the Tabu. The Tuaregs, who traditionally travelled and traded across the most remote regions of the Sahara, were largely known as staunch supporters of the late Colonel. The Tabu – a sub-group of Tuaregs – on the other hand, were long denied many rights under the Gaddafi regime, including the right to citizenship. It was a matter that was rarely spoken of, until 2008 when the southern city of Kufrah's Tabu tribe protested against a lack of access to state healthcare and other rights they had long been denied. Kufrah lies some two thousand kilometres south of Tripoli, close to the Egyptian, Sudanese and Chadian borders. The unrest was met with lethal force and the city was cordoned off by security forces and phone lines were cut-off. There was no way of independently verifying the initial reports that came out of Kufrah and the unrest was quickly covered up by authorities. We – the media – were flown in some two weeks later on a government sponsored tour of the city to show us "there was nothing." The Gaddafi regime only spoke of "skirmishes" due to an enigmatic "dispute between tribes". Libyan opposition websites abroad reported a total of 11 people killed in the clashes between the Tabu and Gaddafi's security forces.

When I went there, I was taken to the dusty town centre where no one dared speak of anything – not even the weather – as the government minders remained close by. In a conference hall in the oasis town, later in the afternoon, the journalists were made to witness a gathering of "representatives of the Tabu tribe" who seemingly only gathered to chant in support of Colonel Gaddafi and deny there were any problems. I left Kufrah with more questions than answers as was so often the case when trying to cover a story in Gaddafi's Libya.

There was a minority ethnic group which I did have plenty of access to however. They were the Amazigh, and they have long waited for their voices to be heard.

Amazigh-Imazighen-Berber

Imagine – for a moment – that you were denied the right to publically state your ethnic roots in your own country, by your own government. Imagine that the state re-defined your ethnic heritage by giving you a new one, and you were unable to object. Can you picture, knowing your ethnic language but not being allowed to speak it unless you were behind closed doors or well away from a fellow national who might be working for the regime you feared most? If you are able to do all that and add decades of psychological repression to it, you may have come close to understanding how many of Libya's Amazigh population lived under Colonel Gaddafi's rule. They are internationally known as Berbers but that is viewed by many as a derogatory term.

There are some thirty million Amazigh in North Africa, mostly concentrated in Morocco and Algeria. Historically, they are the indigenous settlers of this region and above all, they are not Arabs. But as world history has taught us time and again, it is often the indigenous people of a land that are made to feel like illegal immigrants generations later. In modern history, it is similar to the native Indians of America being kicked out by the "The White man".

The Amazigh tribes of North Africa struggled for decades to preserve their cultural heritage and identity long after colonial rule ended throughout the continent. Eventually, they regained many rights in countries like Algeria and Morocco, though they still feel marginalised by their rulers.

Libya under Gaddafi however – always at the forefront of "great change" – saw the Amazigh tribes re-defined by the state. It is unclear precisely when it happened but Colonel Gaddafi declared that Amazigh tribes became extinct long ago, since the days of the Numidia Kingdom and he went on to say that all of them were "Arabs of the pure kind". He also said that Libya is for Libyans and its people should not claim different origins.

Unlike neighbouring countries, the Amazigh of Libya were never allowed to teach their language in schools, speak in the media about their origins, or celebrate their traditional holidays. In the early 1970s, they were even slapped with a name ban to prevent them from using Imazighen names. To be fair, that last bit affected all Libyans because the law stated that Libyans could only use Arab names when naming their children, otherwise they would be barred from registering them in any municipality. The name ban was lifted in September 2005, in theory. The calls for it to be scrapped were made after the Colonel's "reformist" son, Saif Al-Islam Gaddafi toured the western mountains of Libya. The charity foundation he headed declared the law an "infringement on civil liberties". It was the first time many Libyans had ever heard the phrase used here.

Many weeks later, a trusted and well informed source told me that Saif Al-Islam Gaddafi was going to take an increasingly public role, and was being lined up as a potential successor to his father – if and when the Colonel died of course. That proved to be the case. From then on he was widely touted as the "heir-apparent" even though he consistently denied it.

The Amazigh population speak Tamazight – a language that you rarely ever heard in Tripoli. Some would argue that was because the language faded and the new generation of Libyan Amazigh had no knowledge of it. That's true, but it's only part of the story. The reason it faded is because it could not be taught in schools, and that its use in public was banned.

Farther afield in the mountains or in the coastal city of Zuwara, it is an entirely different story. If they trust the people present, they will speak their language freely.

Libya's Amazigh population is concentrated in the western mountains of Yefren and Nafusa and along the coast in Zuwara, not far from the country's borders with Tunisia. Those who moved to Tripoli appeared to accept their roots would have to be hidden, though they would always announce upon first encounter – at least to a foreigner – "We are not Arabs." It is a phrase I grew accustomed to hearing from Libyan Amazigh I met in Tripoli – they had taken it upon themselves to educate the outsider about their identity in case we were too ill-informed to know better.

I recall my first encounter with Faten almost seven years ago. She was a young, feisty, driven woman who came to be a trusted friend over the years. She had lived many years abroad when her father was a diplomat; she spoke Italian, English and Arabic.

"I am Amazighia…Amazigh are NOT Arabs?" she said almost defensively but with a warm, knowing smile.

"I KNOW!" I replied.

On another occasion I recall a discussion with Faten about the mentalities and attitudes of people across Libya, where she promptly concluded:

"The BEST people in Libya are the Amazigh and the people of the east, especially Benghazi"

I had heard that same declaration from eastern Libyans before as well, though naturally they put themselves first in the phrase.

As an observer, the connection between Eastern Libyans and the Amazigh of western Libya are quite obvious; they both felt like kindred spirits – the most punished people in the country under Gaddafi's iron rule. But at times some of them appeared to feel the need to be the "number 1" at something. Sadly, in Libya, the competition was often over which group of people was subjected to the most persecution.

However, I also came across natives of Benghazi and Tripoli who would secretly say they felt "the Berbers are rude and angry people". At which point, I felt like pointing out: "Wouldn't you be if you were as oppressed as them? On top of the usual day-to-day repression that all Libyans face that is."

The "rudeness" was always attributed to the language that is so foreign to the ears of Arab Libyans. Following the Libyan uprising, the Tamazight language and Amazigh identity made a re-appearance. Amidst the red, black and green flags of the rebels who gathered to celebrate liberation, the blue, green and yellow of the Amazigh was frequently raised just as high.

• • •

One of the most poignant events I came across involving the Amazigh in Libya was the first time they were – in theory – allowed to mark their own New Year festival. The world over, it was celebrated on January 12th. The state authorities gave them permission to mark the event one day late. On January 13th, 2008, Libya's Amazigh were to mark their special annual occasion in a public forum in the capital – for the first time in decades. Indeed, there was always a "but" in Muammar Gaddafi's Libya. Officially, it was announced as an occasion that marked the "year of the arrival of the Libyan leader Sheshank", an Amazigh King who historically unified Libya, Egypt, Sudan and the Middle East.

The word Amazigh was not used. The event was marked in the ageing Scouts Theatre in Tripoli with a lively band – a rare sighting here at that time – called *Asin* in Tamazight, meaning The Days. It was the first time I heard Libyans singing in their language here – the sensation resembled the first concert I ever attended but with the added knowledge that the talent was singing for its life, its rights, and its very existence. The commencement of their "show" triggered a halt in the live feed from state television, after the opening remarks that maintained official lines.

The crowd was charged with euphoria although the image was not conventional – can you picture a live band playing to an audience that appeared to be desperate to bounce about but was restricted by a cinema-like seating arrangement on velvety red chairs?

There were some low-level representatives of Gaddafi's government in our midst at the start of the event; they gave long speeches that prompted my exit to the foyer and that of many others in the audience. I was bored, the Amazigh were just angry. The Libyans around me were expressing themselves furiously in Tamazight, shouting in the ash cloud of cigarette smoke that soon engulfed us all.

"Who do you work for?" A man asked me in Arabic, noticing the very large microphone in my hand. "The BBC World Service…no camera, just audio." It was a line I always used in Libya, knowing there were some who would criticise the regime on the condition their face was not seen.

"You are Lebanese or English…OK… good, I want to tell you what's happening so the world knows! I can speak English."

"I'm all ears…and microphone" I jokingly replied now nervous of potential spies in our midst that would grab him if they overheard what appeared to be a very critical remark coming.

Yousef was from Zuwara and he spent a good ten minutes lambasting the government who "want to force me to say I am an Arab," he bitterly explained.

The officials in the theatre had apparently skewed their historical account of Sheshank by referring to him as an Arab king. To the people in that room, it was an unforgivable and enraging statement.

The rant quickly turned into the Arabs vs. the Amazigh of Libya.

He spoke of things I was well aware of at the time and I was grateful that he was brave enough to share it on the record. He explained how "the Arabs had the media" and how the Amazigh people in Libya were not allowed to speak through the state media, that they had no voice and no rights and that they could not even speak of the rights they sought because "it is forbidden".

In another corner by a large stained window a man who appeared to be in anguish stood in a corner. Walking over, I sensed he would not want to speak openly.

"Please no recording, I don't want to be interviewed. I know you're a journalist, I saw you speaking to that man" he said, as I approached.

I shoved my microphone and recorder into an oversized handbag and asked what was wrong because he looked to be on the verge of either tears or a mental breakdown – I was not sure which. After he'd established my nationality, the identity of my employees, and realised that I had a Lebanese dialect which meant I wasn't Libyan, he appeared to relax as he leaned his head against the window. He did not want to talk or be quoted in any way, he wanted to vent to a sympathetic ear. I distinctly recall a barrage of profanity towards the regime and an excessive use of the word "hate". He hated everything: the country, the regime and the people that helped it along the way over the decades. "We are Amazigh! We are not Arabs!" he said in the end, with burning frustration.

Cultural identity becomes ever more attractive and vital when you are denied the right to associate with it.

CHAPTER SEVEN

LIFE GOES ON

Hopeless

One of the first things I noticed about Libyans was that they seemed to have no hope. There was no sense that change was possible or that they could do anything to alter the direction of their lives. Most did not "dream big", or aspire to reach their full potential. They had no aspirations. I imagine it is not uncommon among people living under tyranny. That may be why so many foreign embassy drivers were actually engineering graduates or why I met a young man who sold pirated CDs for a living even though he had degrees in chemical engineering and business studies. He'd already decided it was hopeless to pursue his goals because they wouldn't survive the regime's bureaucracy.

Even so, Libyans were not inclined to flee their country on boats across the Mediterranean, like so many did from neighbouring Tunisia, Morocco and Egypt. Only those who could afford to leave by plane did so.

I came to understand that it was not simply pride that kept many in Libya but also a sense that their situation was not dire enough to prompt them to risk their lives for greener pastures on European shores. Even though there were many families in Tripoli and elsewhere who were as poor as the poorest in the region, the state made sure that most did not go hungry through its handouts and also made certain that most lived without a hope in the world that one day they would be able to lead a more dignified life. This was predominantly the case in the early decades of Gaddafi's rule, but as the country opened up to the West following the state's renouncement of its nuclear weapons programme in 2003, a semblance of normalcy gradually returned to Tripoli and Libya at large.

The foreign companies that filed in absorbed some of the widespread unemployment, but not all. Small and big local businesses increasingly developed in the years that followed and a flicker of hope for better days to come was settling in. Even then, however, many did not feel the changes they then secretly hoped for could ever be realized under Gaddafi's regime – that appeared to be a hopeless case, but not for long.

Nationalism

Most countries in the world are often identified by their people, who act as ambassadors to their homelands. Libya was almost always known to outsiders as the country ruled by Gaddafi; it was especially ingrained in the minds of those looking in from abroad because few visitors roamed the oil-rich country. Tourism was either non-existent for more than a decade or highly restricted for enigmatic reasons by the state even after it normalized its ties with the West. Having a man highly associated with international terrorism represent Libyans was embarrassing to many of the country's nationals.

Libya's post-independence flag under the monarchy came to be one of the key symbols of the country's revolution. It symbolized the independence they sought from a totalitarian regime that ruled them for more than four decades and a figure that came to represent them as a people. With every city or town that fighters opposed to the regime gained control of, the mostly untrained civilian rebels who fought in the conflict staked their "new" flag – the red, black and the green, with a star and crescent in the middle.

Though thousands of Gaddafi's supporters waved green flags in Tripoli during the conflict in 2011, in the years prior to that, I had never seen people wave the national flag, or even speak of it in favourable terms. "Look at it!" my landlady once said, "they (the state) never even use proper material for the flag, it looks like an old dusting rag. I use a nicer cloth to wipe my kitchen counters!"

"We have no nationalism" Libyans often privately said, "we are not proud to be Libyans. We are proud by nature as individuals, but not as a nation, Gaddafi took that away from us". It was perhaps because, as the late Colonel himself put it in February 2011:

> *They want no identification, identity when they say to people, Libya in Lebanon. When they say Libya, Revolution, Libya, Qaddafi, all African nations consider us, as the Mecca, rulers of the world, even the superpowers, they want to converge on Benghazi, on Tripoli.*

The point he perhaps incoherently tried to make was that he, Muammar Gaddafi, put Libya on the map. It is true, much of the world did not know where Libya was, some had never heard of it. Young Libyans who travelled to the West carried tales of how foreigners or even immigration officers in Canada or the US would answer back and say "What? You mean Lebanon? Or Liberia?" However, as soon as they uttered the word "Gaddafi", the confusion was cleared – "Oh LIBYA,

Gaddafi Libya" was the frequent reaction. Is it any wonder that many Libyans at times felt stateless?

So many could not even relate to the national anthem of their country under Gaddafi – "It sounds like the Egyptian anthem", or "It's the old Egyptian national anthem about Arab unity, Gaddafi imposed it on us when he dreamt of uniting the Arab World" they would say. It was actually a former Egyptian marching song, called Allahu Akbar, or God is greatest, and sang against "aggression of the oppressor". It was a song that was held in high regard during the Suez Canal War in 1956.

Since the Libyan uprising in 2011, not only was Libya's post-independence flag raised (the one used under the monarchy), but people also began singing the original national anthem, *Libya Libya Libya*. Like the flag, the anthem had meaning to the nation and to the people – it spoke of Libya's struggle for independence and honoured its national people. Many of this generation of Libyans who grew up without ever hearing it, unlike their elders, have since learnt it and voluntarily sing it in public or in their homes or even play it as a music track in their cars. The sense of a new-found nationalism is helping bind together post-Gaddafi Libya.

Saif Al-Islam Gaddafi seemingly recognized the issue in the early days of the uprising in his now infamous first televised address on the 20th of February, the night the mass anti-government protests reached the capital for the first time.

> *Before we let weapons come between us, from tomorrow, in 48 hours, we will call for a new conference for new laws. We will call for new media laws, civil rights, lift the stupid punishments, we will have a constitution... We will have a new Libya, new flag, and new anthem.*

> *Or else, be ready to start a civil war and be ready for chaos and forget the oil and petrol.*
> Saif Al-Islam, February 20th, state TV recorded address.

That was after he remarked that most of the protestors were drunk, drugged or Islamists. That aside, the promise of all things "new" were ultimately forty two years late.

Nationalism is not only shaped by the flag or the anthem and a people's pride in them. It is gained through generations of historical struggle, the achievements of a nation and that of its people. Libyans were only ever proud of Omar Al-Mokhtar, the historical figure they saw as the country's national hero who stood up to his Italian colonial masters till the day he was hanged by them in 1931. It was the memory of Omar Al-Mokhtar that was invoked as Libyans took to the streets to face their dictator and his armed men. It was the flag and the Libyan national anthem under the monarchy of King Idriss that they waved and sang with every day that passed. Meanwhile Gaddafi's supporters simply chanted, "God, Muammar and Libya, that's it!"

Life Goes On...

It may appear that Libyans lived every moment of their lives in fear and worry of what the days or years would bring. Some perhaps did, but overall life does go on even in the worst of dictatorships. It is perhaps why Libya's popular uprising was almost forty-two years in the making. Endurance was a way of life here, and that is what gave Libyans the strength just to "get on with it". Like any other country, society functioned with all its pros and cons. Libyans only remembered the ills of the regime when they were asked about it or when they were in a reflective mood amongst friends or family they trusted. The challenges of daily life were all there. The joys at the newborn or a new marriage or the graduating son or daughter or the success of a new business (when they were allowed to open them) all existed. So too did the Libyan operating system we came to know as IBM.

Should you ever decide to visit the country or consider working in Libya, be mindful of what any number of revolutions is unlikely to conquer. IBM is the English acronym that came to define the prevalent business and social culture in Libya. It refers to the Arabic *Inshallah, Bokra, Ma'alesh*, or God-willing, Tomorrow, It's OK! It's a term that the expat community in Libya coined to describe their obstacles at work; partly to shed light on the bureaucracy and at times the laziness of state employees or even their own.

In the early years of my work here I could not tolerate it; it infuriated, confused and frustrated me. I am a Muslim myself and quite aware that we often say "God-willing" or *Inshallah* when we speak of any future plans; but having grown up in the West, it was slightly – an understatement here – unnerving when making an appointment for work or waiting for an official letter to be written and stamped, to simply be told *Inshallah*.

"You mean yes?" I would often question.

"*Inshallah.*"

"So 10:00am?"

"*Inshallah.*"

Come appointment day and by noon you will realize what *Inshallah* means. It would often be that or a "*bokra*" ("tomorrow")… followed by a sympathetic "*Ma'alesh.*" ("It's okay!") The cycle sometimes repeated itself for days on end.

Libyans lead a more laid-back Mediterranean lifestyle than any other country along this coast. Like Spain and Italy, it is a common trait shared by countries in the Med. It is, however, taken to new heights in this North African State. Private shops open from around 11am – 2pm, followed by an extended siesta until six in the evening when they open shop again. Like their fallen leader of forty-two years, they very much functioned more at night than during the day.

In the years I have been here since 2004, which are largely seen as "the good years", life may have been abnormal in "my reporting world" in the first twenty-four months or so, but like Libyans I began to see past the troubles and beyond the painful stories so many shared. I even came to forget that my phone was in all likelihood religiously tapped or that all my emails were read by someone out there in Tripoli who worked for the security apparatus. The "spies" around Tripoli started going by unnoticed too; like the Colonel's pictures, they were a permanent feature of the landscape that simply became old, boring and invisible to the naked eye. Being rudely interrupted by a man in civilian clothes as I occasionally recorded on a public street and then stalled for hours until he "verified who I was" with some mysterious person on the other end of his phone, transformed from an exasperating occurrence to a minor annoyance that was at times laughable over the years.

In the summer, Libyan families spent many of the weekends camping on the beach as expats hunted for the best and most discrete locations along Libya's pristine and largely untouched Mediterranean shores. Some Libyan men who appeared to have an unusual liking for the "wrestler's look" would parade up and down the coast with their bulging muscles and popping veins peeking through tight jean shorts and a t-shirt about two sizes too small. There were also the jet skiers of Tripoli who appeared to care little for the safety of civilians as they dangerously sped past close to shore. Young Libyan lovers would shyly – though rarely – stroll along these very shores or sit in small discreet corners of a public park holding hands. The men who dominated society would hug their morning, evening and night macchiato outside the many small coffee stands or shops. They especially made their presence known with their lethal driving that at times appeared to make up for what seemed like their lack of political drive. It was that or the relatively new trend that developed in 2009 with the motorcycling exhibitionists of the country who entertained car drivers on the highways or motorways by blocking the traffic to make way for their tricks. Or they spent hours a day aimlessly driving up and down the main roads of popular residential districts like Gergaresh and Ben Ashour, staring at each other to see who was out, or hoping to get a smile or a phone number from a woman to their liking as they shouted their mobile numbers out of the window.

There was the aspiring guitarist that played his instrument at private gatherings behind closed doors, and the unpopular break dancers in Tripoli who performed for a rarely present audience. Libyan painters even found their way back again into Libya's arts arena in recent years, with the occasional small exhibitions around the capital that often only attracted a small audience of expats in the community. Above all, there was the year-round weekly gathering of good friends or families who exchanged stories, laughed, sang or even danced within the confines of each other's homes.

Libyan women were not always so far behind, even though they lacked any imposing presence in public. Some are professionals in the workplace although still a glaring minority. Others are the secret caterers of Libyan food and sweet bakes for the more privileged in society; a skill perfected throughout the international sanctions period and long before then when private shops and businesses were closed down in socialist Libya. The majority, however, are the quiet housewives that many did not see, or the daughters that were scarcely visible. Following the Libyan uprising, I recall thinking to myself "where did all these women and young girls come from?" as waves of them descended on parts of Liberation Square in Benghazi at the start of protests and in Martyrs' square in Tripoli several months later when the capital fell. I cannot begin to describe the scenes following the death of the Colonel and declaration of Libya's complete liberation on October 23rd, 2011.

CHAPTER EIGHT

THE MEDIA BUBBLE

I was once asked by a visiting colleague from the BBC to describe a typical evening on Libya's state television channel. I jokingly replied that the information he sought would require me to actually watch it.

On a normal day, the state-run channel *Al-Jamahiriyah* would broadcast a news bulletin in Arabic, and sometimes a single report on Gaddafi would occupy the entire edition. On other occasions there would be no script, no words, just a stream of footage showing the Colonel shaking hands with guests as they sat in his tent at the Bab Al-Aziziyah compound.

For some light relief there would be "soap operas" from Syria or Egypt, but they would be interspersed with occasional freeze-frame images of the Green Book accompanied by a "voice of god" reading a passage from it.

There were also some "talk shows" where they would interview a government official who would link every answer to Gaddafi and his Green Book. My personal favourite was a slot for Tunisian or Libyan singers where they would stand and sing in front of a backdrop of mountains or desert. One night, I remember a man standing in a forest wearing a 1990s suit and tie with big shades. The tune resembled a lullaby.

Libyan media was entirely dominated by the state; private media was illegal. When in doubt, refer to Green Book, p. 38:

Democratically, a natural person should not be permitted to own any means of publication of information. However he has the natural right to express himself by any means even if it is an irrational manner to prove his madness.

And so it was that anyone who expressed dissent in public could be dismissed by the regime as "mad", before they were imprisoned, tortured or killed. Two infamous cases include the late dissident Fathi Jahmi who had "psychological problems" according to Gaddafi's officials. He was jailed, and then released under house arrest, and eventually died in a hospital in Jordan. Then there was Iman Al-Obedi. She was the woman who, at the start of the uprising, stormed into a hotel in Tripoli where foreign journalists were staying, and screamed that she'd been raped by Gaddafi forces. She was accused by the government spokesman – Moussa Ibrahim – of having mental problems. Then she was "a drunkard", and finally it was suggested she might be a prostitute.

The regime had more trouble dismissing the thousands who took to the streets at the start of the protests. They couldn't all be mad. So, instead they were branded pill-popping youths who were on a diet of hallucinogenic tablets.

Some years after my arrival in Tripoli, Colonel Gaddafi's favoured son, Saif Al-Islam, launched the One Nine Media Company and the first alternative to state television: the Al-Libiyah Satellite channel. Then he added more channels, and introduced two newspapers and a news agency. All were technically state media though, and despite a fleeting attempt to "push the boundaries", they soon pedalled the normal state propaganda. In 2011, his TV network became one of many the state relied on to disseminate false information and implant a sense of inescapable fear amongst the people.

• • •

I was once informed by a Lebanese colleague from the Arab news channel, Alarabiya, that "on a white-washed wall, if there is even the smallest speck of black, your attention will be drawn to it – it stands out." Over the years I came to view myself as that speck on a clear Libyan canvas.

The journalist who made the comment was trying to comfort me after a bruising encounter with the Libyan authorities. I had just walked out of a telling-off from the head of the Foreign Press Office whom we shall call Mr Grumpy. (Even now it would be unfair to give his real name, or that of any other low-ranking officials. Most should be allowed a chance to rebuild their lives under the new regime. Naming them would only provoke unnecessary hostility). Mr Grumpy was unhappy – to put it mildly – with a story I had done for radio that also made its way to BBC online. The Foreign Press Office in Tripoli was every foreign journalist's visa to enter the country for a brief visit. Any request went through them first and they were the ones who approved or rejected an application sent through the *people's bureau* from abroad.

The "crime" was a single quote I'd taken from a Libyan who worked at a record store selling cassette tapes. I was working on a story about the improving ties with the West and the oil deals, and I'd tried to get some reaction from normal citizens on the street. This particular young man felt the changes did not make a difference to the people because they did not see the benefits of the oil wealth.

That single line he uttered was apparently the dark speck on a white wall that my Lebanese colleague referred to.

I was confronted with the apparent scandalous comment in black and white – quite literally. Mr Grumpy had a printed copy of the online article in hand as proof, waving it around through a blur of insults directed at me, the BBC and the foreign media at large. It was 2004 and was my first real confrontation with the "powers that be". As a novice at the job and in a country that was meant to be my post for the next few years, I did not know what to make of his fury.

"So you're saying the state is CORRUPT?!" he angrily demanded.

I did not specifically say that however my interviewee alluded to it.

"No?" I replied in a rather inquisitive tone which sparked more fury.

"WHO TOLD YOU THIS?!" he demanded.

Well that's just silly, I thought to myself. I don't actually know the individual's name, he was a random voice representing an opinion. Why is he questioning my speaker's character?

"It's just an opinion" I hit back and embarked on a speech of my own with a technical, no-nonsense explanation of how the BBC editorial policy worked and that when needed and when possible we included people's opinions on a story.

"AH? WHAT DO YOU MEAN PEOPLE'S OPINION?!… People's opinion!"

Clearly there was a problem with having an opinion. I was repeatedly asked where this man with an opinion was. I knew exactly where of course because I spoke to him at his place of work after many unsuccessful attempts to get a voice elsewhere in public. This is it, I thought to myself at the time – my first test. This is where protecting my sources would be diligently adhered to. I had read about it in school, and in my one week of training at the BBC before coming out to Libya, and seen it in movies. I knew exactly how to handle it.

"I don't know!" I lied.

I don't recall exactly how that conversation ended but I do recall being threatened with possible deportation and accused of many "unprofessional" deeds and I remember my eyes welling up. I needed to make a quick exit. He saw my face and I despised him for it.

In all likelihood, I got away with about 90% of my reporting from Libya because it was for radio and the regime's "foreign media monitors" apparently didn't listen to BBC World Service's English radio output. I probably would have been tossed out or possibly "killed in an accident" if the state actually heard the rare critical voices that made it to air.

There were other similar incidents over the months and early years of my work here; times where I would walk out of the dreaded Foreign Press Office close to tears. One event that I will never forget was probably the closest I got to being shipped out and blacklisted from Gaddafi's Libya for life.

It was the first time I've ever broken down and wept uncontrollably. I was shaking with the emotion of it all.

The story in question was an opinion piece (my own reflections) on a topic I suggested for the World Service's Christmas stockpot; that is the time many correspondents are asked to file a variety of light or serious pieces to wrap-up the year gone by or to look ahead. It was New Year's Eve when one of the world's biggest tragedies hit – the Asian Tsunami.

I had pitched a story about "what the country you are based in should give up in the New Year" category. I suggested a light-hearted take on the "Secret Service". That was, with hindsight, a colossal mistake for someone who is based in a dictatorship as a correspondent and not just passing through as all the other foreign reporters were at the time. Where does one begin with this tale?

I was happily skipping around a friend's home, before heading out to celebrate my first New Year in Libya with new friends and a new life. We were to attend the New Caledonian Society's bash. Then my mobile phone rang, and Mr Grumpy's name flashed up. I naively assumed he was going to wish me well on the eve of a New Year.

"Happy New Year!" I beamed.

"Happy New Year? What happy new year? What are you doing? What have you done? What's this…" it went on for a good minute.

I was genuinely confused; I had no idea what he was talking about because I had filed that story two weeks prior to its broadcast and had practically forgotten about it. Through the incessant shouting, I could barely understand what he was rambling on about and then I finally understood.

At first he angrily told me to pack my bags and that I was to leave on the first flight out. Oddly, all I thought at that precise moment was "my career in journalism is over." Of course it would not have been but I did not want to get kicked out of Libya, what was the point? Who would tell the Libyan story? Another minute passed with more shouting from the other end of the line; another thought developed "the *mukhabarat* (secret service) will assassinate me tonight or tomorrow." Then he hung up on me. I had barely gotten two words in at the beginning, and that was that.

Terror is a mild term to describe the roller-coaster of emotions that followed. I felt light-headed, the palms of my hands were sweating, I was hot and shaking. I called the office and practically screamed down the line, ordering a colleague of mine at the African Service to check if the story was posted on BBC online and instructing her that, if it was, she needed to get rid of it immediately. I would not have dreamt of doing that if it was a news story carrying testimony from Libyans. But this was not. These were my own personal reflections which had put me directly in the firing line.

"It's not online" my colleague replied. "Give me a minute, calm down and I'll find out where it was broadcast and call you back."

Five or ten minutes later I was informed that it had gone out on the Arabic service; the one radio outlet that was religiously monitored by the Libyan authorities.

"Rana do you feel unsafe?" my colleague asked

Of course I felt unsafe! I had already envisaged myself hanging in the main square in front of a crowd.

"Stay at a friend's place for the night if it's possible, don't stay alone at your apartment."

"I'll be fine" I replied with an effort at composure.

The African service editor at the time, Joseph Warungu, called me soon after. We all seemingly went into crisis mode. He suggested he speak with Mr Grumpy. I initially thought it was a bad idea, afraid that officials would become even angrier, but there seemed no other option. So Joseph spoke with him and called me back about half an hour later. I had calmed down by then, the hysteria had subsided. My editor reported the same type of phone call; shouting followed by a long lecture, but he informed me that Mr Grumpy wanted to meet me the following day and said that, by the end of the conversation he had calmed down somewhat.

I went out that night to usher in the New Year in a miserable state and stayed with friends. I spent the early morning hugging a toilet bowl – nerves, I think.

There was an audience this time – just one person, a tall softly spoken Omar Sherif (not the actor) – a man I liked because he was a calm and friendly character who listened to complaints made by foreign hacks with a nod and a smile. He worked in the Foreign Press Office, sometimes as a minder and other times as the head administrator.

He occasionally tried to coolly convey what Mr Grumpy was trying to tell me through his temper, as though I didn't understand. I noticed Omar covering a discreet smirk as I responded to allegations of misrepresenting the secret service and of calling Libya "a police state". This wasn't the time to explain how accurate I'd been, or to point out that he was demonstrating it right now with this very meeting. Instead I explained my story had been intended to merely paint a picture of how the secret service looked, dressed, moved, lounged around in hotel receptions, and how some in Libya said half the population worked for security. I had suggested, in the piece, that Libya's New Year resolution should be to do away with them because there were too many and most appeared useless. It was supposed to be light-hearted. I was young and carefree and had missed the fact that they knew where I lived, what I ate, what I read, and who I befriended.

It was a long session. In summary, at first he threatened to sue me. Then he threatened to sue the BBC. Then he told me to apologize. I did not of course. Then he suggested I sign a paper stating that what I did was wrong; at which point I informed him that I did not own the BBC and could not sign anything on their behalf.

I thought it might go to our legal department, the state of Libya vs. the BBC. How would that play out in court? Could we prove that the suit-clad dodgy Libyans who slouched and smoked in hotel receptions were secret service men? Or that the equally seedy looking men who sat in parked cars all day across the city were spooks? More importantly, would any Libyan testify to support the claim in a court of law? Unlikely!

Mr Grumpy cursed and shouted. I was tired of it all. That's when I broke into tears. I wanted to leave his office. I wanted to leave his country. I wanted to leave the profession altogether. At this point, his mood began to ease slightly. He told me to stop crying, and there may even have been a flicker of sympathy, even though his words remained harsh. It was my fault, he said, I had written the offending words and I was causing trouble for myself. I cried even harder. Eventually he told me to leave the office and informed me that I was no longer allowed to work, for the foreseeable future. My accreditation was not withdrawn but I was indefinitely suspended. That lasted almost two weeks. I didn't even leave the apartment. Then, I received a call inviting me to an event where the Colonel was going to issue an address. It was their way of saying "the ban is now lifted". Life and work returned to "normal", until the next incident that was.

A Libyan friend later said to me, "Rana, you have to understand that someone from Gaddafi's inner circle probably called and shouted at him first". I tried to imagine the scene: Mr Grumpy, an ageing, intelligent man well into his sixties, fluent in at least four languages, being rebuked and insulted over the phone because a young foreigner insulted his country.

Months later, after further shouting incidents, I was at peace with his actions – the sobbing replaced with silent anger.

The most common "offence" committed by journalists included not turning up for a news event in which Colonel Gaddafi was to make an appearance. News events of this kind never had a schedule. We would be called at any hour of the day or night and informed "You must be at the Foreign Press Office in half an hour and we will take you all (the journalists) by bus" or "You must be at the airport in twenty minutes" (most commonly for a flight to Sirte).

After the first dozen occasions of rushing off to mystery locations without even knowing the story, and then being forced to wait for up to seven hours before an official would tell you what was going on, most of the press corps either developed a sense of humour about it or rebelled. 70% of the time, there was no newsworthy story at all. 25% of the time, one was better off staying home to listen to the Live Feed of Gaddafi's speech and working on it from there.

During my first two years in Libya, my attendance record was almost flawless, even though 60% of the time I did not file a story because the event was purely propaganda. The few times I missed an event were mostly due to circumstances beyond my control. For example, the taxi driver I know and trust was unable to pick me up at 11pm at such short notice and, as a woman, I could not just hop into a random cab at night. I may have faked a cold once or twice too. All non-attendance was carefully noted by the Foreign Press Office and often threatened with "This is the second time, he (Mr Grumpy) will be very angry with you." Or if Mr. Grumpy saw you the next time, he would scowl and remind you that "you are not doing your job" and threaten to withdraw accreditation. Two years later I cut classes – pardon me, events – quite often, particularly the large over-crowded ones on the annual anniversaries that were marked in the dead of night with thousands of Gaddafi "supporters" bused in to cheer for their Colonel. There were quite a few. I rebelled in my own small world. Mr Grumpy appeared to tolerate me by then and a silent peace treaty was signed – though it was at times broken. By the third year I was called "my daughter" a few times as well.

Till this day, I am not entirely certain that he was a die-hard Gaddafi loyalist at all. He retired some years ago to be replaced by someone we'll call Mr "New". He was an overall nicer man and kept himself to himself. I last contacted Mr. Grumpy almost a year before my April 2010 wedding, just to say hello and to ask about his health. He congratulated me on my upcoming wedding and wished me all the best after ranting on for a few minutes about how happy he was to hear from me and rebuking me for not calling him earlier. He still likened me to "a daughter".

With the death of Gaddafi and his regime I cannot help but wonder whether he is mourning the man who was once his leader and the regime he supported or whether he's regretting all the lost time working in a system that probably drained him of every ounce of pleasantness he once possessed.

CHAPTER NINE

PRELUDE TO A REVOLUTION

When an average person's phone rings in the middle of a working week at some ungodly hour past midnight it is assumed there must be an emergency of sorts, involving a friend or relative. When a foreign correspondent's phone rings at exactly the same time, it's like someone's tiptoed into the room, crouched beside your sleeping ear, and bellowed at the top of their voice "FIRE!" If it happens at a time when two neighbouring countries have just erupted and overthrown their long-standing rulers, and the international media is relentlessly exploring the possibility of a domino effect tearing right across the region and directly through your patch, then the sensation is exponentially magnified. Before you've even ripped the phone from its charger, there's the rush of guilt; guilt that you're not out there already...whatever the story you should be out there now, on the streets, filing for every conceivable outlet. There is guilt that you were even asleep at all...that you might have missed a seismic event right outside your own window...that this was the very reason you were deployed here in the first place, yet at the critical moment you were lost to the world. Then there is a sense of shame that your editor might have heard the news from a rival network first...that the world's media are already surging across the border to get there before you...that your news-desk is going to have to break the story to you instead of the other way around. But mostly the feeling is one of embarrassment; embarrassment that the biggest story of your life is possibly breaking and you are standing in the middle of your apartment in pyjamas.

That morning in the confusion of interrupted sleep, just two possibilities came to mind: either Colonel Gaddafi was dead or, and this would have been entirely implausible just weeks before, somewhere in Libya a protest had begun.

I had been living with the possibility of the first assumption from the day I moved to this country as the BBC correspondent in February 2004. Within weeks of arriving in Tripoli, I heard that Gaddafi was ill. It turned out to be untrue. The same story resurfaced some time later, and vanished just as quickly. I soon realised these were groundless rumours. Perhaps they were expressions of optimism, but also of anxiety from a nation that had tolerated Gaddafi for decades but was not entirely sure what the country would replace him with if he were to suddenly die.

Much like the rest of the country, I never seriously entertained the prospect of a protest erupting against the Libyan regime until the world witnessed the quick demise of Tunisia's Zine Al-Abidine Ben Ali and Egypt's Hosni Mubarak at the start of 2011. Even then, there were doubts the scenario could possibly be repeated in Libya. By then I had spent enough years in the country to know and understand the levels of fear induced by Gaddafi's secret police. To communicate any kind of dissent, even within the family unit, was far too much of a risk. There could be no repeat of the uprisings here, or so I thought towards the end of January.

In addition to that, there seemed to be some broad acceptance that the country was gradually changing course. Since December 2003 it had begun edging itself out of the deep freeze

– the clichéd expression "came in from the cold" really does no justice in Gaddafi's case. After years of international sanctions prompted by Muammar Gaddafi's sponsorship of international terrorism, the intelligence services of Britain and America had made tentative approaches to their counterparts in Tripoli. They'd manage to cajole out of the Colonel an agreement to give up his clandestine nuclear weapons programme. In return, according to documents found in former Tripoli intelligence offices, Britain and America had begun enthusiastically handing over intelligence on the regime's opponents living abroad. And so, by the spring of 2004, the Colonel had become the West's newly tamed dictator, a cartoon villain with colourful costumes and a taste for female bodyguards. Crucially though, he was no longer seen as a threat. In fact, all this had come about because of Gaddafi's succinct awareness that, if he didn't change, the world's giants could eventually chase him just as they had done Saddam in Iraq. This was a way out.

Muammar Gaddafi had removed any potential excuse for an international attack against Libya. It was a clever and timely move that made all parties look good. The West had won over a former tyrant and, in doing so, had opened up his vast reserves of oil and gas to the rest of the world, whilst Gaddafi had won new friends in the grubby world of intelligence-sharing, and had successfully batted away the damaging international sanctions.

Meanwhile, inside Libya itself, people were largely left with the old text of a past and present that was ultimately unforgivable. What governments in the West perhaps conveniently missed – as is so often the case in their love-hate relationships with dictators across the globe – is the internal hardships of the people whose bitter and brutal experiences continued as the outside world looked away. Irrespective of the Arab Spring that swept the region and encouraged many to transform their fears into direct action, it is the memories of the dead, the oppressed, and the shunned that ultimately sparked the Libyan uprising.

Revolution, "Civil War", or Nato War?

From my perspective, inside the country, no one could have anticipated the turn to arms and subsequent full-scale war. Paradoxically for the regime, it was only possible because of its vast stockpiles of armaments kept at locations across the country. By "vast" I do mean inexplicably excessive. It was no wonder perhaps that Saif Al-Islam Gaddafi – the LSE educated son of the Colonel – announced in the early days of the uprising that they had bombed weapons depots on the outskirts of the capital and elsewhere. The regime had found itself in the bizarre position of having to destroy its own armaments, in case they fell into rebel hands. This was after the entire eastern region – from Benghazi to Tobruk – had already fallen into the hands of civilian protestors and young men had helped themselves at arms depots formerly controlled by the regime. Now they were merrily running around with Rocket Propelled Grenade launchers and AK 47s slung around their necks.

It would have been a foreseeable scenario if there had been an overt opposition group in the country, with access to weapons, or if this had been a military coup. In fact, the state had, for many years, wanted Libyans to believe that almost everyone in the country was armed. It was all part of the Alice-in-Wonderland propaganda to make it appear that the people were in charge of their own destiny.

There were only two groups permanently armed: a small number of tribes which had almost unquestioning allegiance to the Colonel and, more importantly, senior members of Gaddafi's Revolutionary Committee Movement that had thousands of members in every city, town and village in Libya.

At the start of the Nato bombing campaign, only Gaddafi's military instillations and weapons caches were targeted. The plan was simple; to deprive the regime of what it relied upon to stay in power. Given the hectic opening weeks of the Nato attacks, and the high volume of targets destroyed, many wrongfully assumed it would be over in weeks. But, as the months went by it seemed the regime had an infinite number of armaments. People – including myself – were in awe when, for example, Nato bombed what's been described as the "largest weapons depot in Africa". And it wasn't in Tripoli. It was at a military base in one of Libya's smallest villages on the outskirts of the western mountain of Nalut. There, stored meticulously inside dozens of underground bunkers, were weapons that dated back to the early 1970s. There were Soviet-era Scud missiles, Italian ignition fuses, weapons from China and Spain, ammunition for high-calibre machine guns, and a whole bunker containing sticks of dynamite. It was as though the Colonel had spent the last forty-two years of his rule preparing for urban warfare against the world.

Whilst equipping himself so comprehensively on the ground though, Gaddafi had allowed his firepower in other areas to decay. The Libyan air force was largely run-down, and capable of carrying out just a few missions inside the country. Even then, its bombing was mercifully inaccurate, either because the aircrews were so poorly trained, or more likely because they had taken a principled and courageous decision to miss the targets they'd been ordered to destroy. Two of his fighter pilots went a stage further. They were scrambled to attack demonstrators in Benghazi just days into the uprising. Instead they turned their F1 Mirage planes towards the Mediterranean Sea, and headed for Malta, defecting rather than killing their own people. The pair only returned when the fighting ended six months later. Two other pilots who tried the same thing, but chose Algeria instead of Malta, were not so fortunate. They were returned to Libya and are said to have been executed.

• • •

During those early days of the Nato bombing, I was alarmed to hear so much opposition from experts and politicians living outside the country. Most of them invoked Iraq and Afghanistan as examples of what would befall Libya as a result of Western intervention. I accept it has often been the case that such military interventions have either been botched, unnecessary or simply useless. However, the view is very different when you are living inside the country in question. Without foreign intervention, we knew it was far less likely Gaddafi could be overthrown. He had effectively "coup-proofed" himself: creating layer after layer of secret police whose job it was not only to monitor the general population, but to keep an eye on each other. Divisions within the army were similar, so that any germ of disloyalty within the ranks would be spotted and extinguished. So, Libyans could not have reached anywhere near a tipping point without Nato.

Then there's the issue of why, with all the attendant health warnings, did Nato decide to act, and with such enthusiasm? If, as many people believe, the underlying cause for becoming embroiled militarily in another country's affairs is often geopolitical rather than humanitarian, then Libyans were extremely fortunate. They were, and of course still are, sitting on a lake of oil. In fact Libya has the largest proven oil reserves in Africa.

Beyond that, Gaddafi was never really a true ally of the West. That would have complicated things further. He was merely someone who was tolerated. His re-entry into the world community had not come about because he'd improved his record on human rights inside his own country. The West cannot have genuinely believed that. The relationship was far more self-serving: it was, to borrow from Lyndon B. Johnson, better to have him inside the tent pissing out, than outside the tent pissing in. And so the decision to intervene was made simpler.

The reality is that had Nato held back, if the no-fly zone had not been imposed and had the West not – as many observed – made a swift decision to get rid of Gaddafi for good, Libyans would have been engaged in a prolonged and bloody civil war. It would have claimed the lives of an inestimable number of innocent civilians, surrounded in Benghazi by Gaddafi's tanks, or caught up in cross-fire or murdered for their suspected support for the rebels. Many more would have died after daring to take up arms – and they too, or course, would have been civilians.

It would have been a deep-seated, slow burning civil war. Both sides – the regime and the majority of the population who despised it – were fighting for something over which there could be no compromise. From early on it was clear that things could never return to the status quo, or even an improved version of it. The turning point for me and most others inside Libya, was when Gaddafi's men fired at unarmed protestors in Benghazi, Libya's second largest city. The protestors were mainly young men: students, doctors, lawyers who marched towards the city's military barracks, the *Katiba*. The regime responded by sending in teams of armed mercenaries who began shooting in cold blood. Then, the army unleashed a terrifying assault, firing randomly into the crowds, and even using anti-aircraft guns.

The regime had committed mass killings before but never in the face of a popular uprising, and never in a context where similar protests in the region had already led to the overthrow of two long-serving leaders. But the real game-changer this time was something Gaddafi and his fighters had no idea how to counter: social networking and video-sharing had taken hold. As the young men of Benghazi took more and more casualties, they were rushing back to their apartments and putting out mobile phone images of the killing which could be seen around the world. Tactical planning was taking place over Facebook. Protestors were exchanging information about what was happening in different parts of the city. There were even suggestions about what to do next from Libyans living in exile. Gaddafi tried to put a block on Facebook, but the youngsters always found a way around it, using proxy sites, the details of which spread quickly across the city. They were always one step ahead. It meant, this time, Gaddafi's crimes could not be covered up.

For the residents of Benghazi and all other Libyans who were about to follow suit, there was no going back. We all knew it. Under Gaddafi, taking to the streets in such a fashion could only attract one punishment: execution. The regime would not have rested before "cleansing" territories of those it believed had defied it. Put simply it was a "do or die" predicament for both sides.

Libyans were largely silent for almost forty-two years, they knew their dictator and his henchmen well and they believed that the only way to deal with their predicament was to take up arms against the regime. They were probably right. Gaddafi and his clan would never have taken the long view. They would never have stood by patiently and waited for the Benghazi protests to burn themselves out. We all knew they could only meet such an event with iron and fire. Neither, once the protests had spread, could he and his seven power-hungry children step aside and hand power to someone else. These options just weren't in his psyche. As one Libyan put it, "Ben-Ali and Mubarak had some class and their countries were functioning states, however corrupt they were; we just had Gaddafi and his family and their worshippers."

In the end, this was a revolution and not a civil war. It was not one side fighting another; Left fighting Right or Believers fighting Unbelievers. Of course Libyans do have their differences, but most reject the suggestion they fought each other. Instead they fought against an absolute authority and ideology that had long suffocated them.

The First Three Days.

On the 18th of February I realised my phone was strangely silent. I was becoming concerned, so I tried calling Afaf, a close friend who was the bureaux chief for AFP (*Agence France Presse*) in Tripoli. All I got was a pre-recorded message effectively saying the call was not allowed. It was a chilling moment. Blocking a phone in Libya usually meant that the line had been monitored by the regime, because that individual was suspected of dissent. It had already happened to some of my contacts in Benghazi, people who had previously kept me up-to-date on the uprising there.

So, I asked my husband to use his phone, and call another AFP correspondent to see if he was having problems getting through to Afaf as well. "No", the friend said, "I've just been speaking to her, all is fine."

"But", he went on, "I was trying to call Rana earlier and could not get through to her, is she OK?"

It was only then that it dawned on us; my number was the one that had been blocked.

I made my way to the *Agence France Presse* office to mix with the only other journalists in Tripoli whom I trusted. I hoped it would help calm my nerves. I had to tell my employer, the BBC, what had happened of course. There were some deliberations back in London. Then, a decision was made that I should lie low. It was too dangerous to carry on broadcasting, they said.

I recall spending the rest of the day at the AFP office in Hay El-Andalous district, an upper middle-class neighbourhood, with Afaf and her colleague. We discussed the events in Benghazi all day, exploring the possible scenarios that would follow, particularly in Tripoli. By 7pm Afaf decided to leave. It was decided I would accompany her back home before returning to mine.

It was already dark when we left and I recall feeling a chill as we stepped outside. I was shaking. It was a cold night but the tremors were not from that – I felt queasy. As we exited the parking area to turn into the main road, our vehicle was forced to break suddenly. A car was speeding down the opposite lane of traffic, followed by another one with a young man sprawled across the windshield and bonnet. Beneath him I could make out a huge poster of Colonel Gaddafi.

We drove down Al-Jamahiriyah (state of the masses) street, near the roundabout that leads into airport road and the Bab Al-Aziziyah compound – Colonel Gaddafi's then residence or rather military headquarters in the capital. On that road, clusters of young people were standing along the pavement. It wasn't a particularly unusual scene but it felt different for whatever reason. It felt as though these young men were waiting in anticipation of a "grand" event. I recall thinking to myself, "Are they the faces of the revolution? Will they be the ones that take to the streets eventually?" It may have been that they were – given the events that unfolded the following night and the number of youths killed on that street alone.

Back at my place, the night was spent fretting – yet again – over the unknown and an instinctive urge to broadcast again on the ongoing events in Benghazi. My husband erupted. He didn't want me to take the risk. His screaming and scolding eventually turned into tears. He was afraid not only for my safety, but for that of his mother and his siblings in the eastern part of the capital and his extended family and father who were all in Benghazi.

"You want to WORK again!?!" he shouted.

"If I don't, who will?!" I hit back through my own tears. I thought he would back down. I really did believe I had spent enough years in Libya by then to understand the parameters of what the regime was capable of. That was a mistake.

My husband is a tall, dignified and striking figure, at least in my eyes. But here he was standing before me in tears of rage.

"Do you know who or what you are dealing with?! Don't you understand?! No one openly reported on the story in the international media from INSIDE the country except for you.

THEY BLOCKED YOUR NUMBER, don't you get it?!!" he said.

I simultaneously did and did not.

"Are you CRAZY?! How can you be so selfish?" he continued.

Tears were streaming down his face. I was, of course, bawling at that stage.

"Do you know what they are capable of? This is all happening in Benghazi. I am from Benghazi! WE are in TRIPOLI, nothing has happened here yet and you want to report on a story that you know they are trying to cover-up by preventing journalists from going there. They have death brigades in this country for people like you. They did it in the 80s and 90s, and they will do it again. They will not think twice about coming here and taking you. They're animals!!! They will drag you out in front of me and execute you! What will I do then?! TELL ME what will I DO?!!!"

Almost as an afterthought, he later added that they would probably execute him as well.

How I felt after that remains something of a blur. I do however remember feeling helpless, angry, and still very much in love all at once as I stared into the face of the man I had married less than a year before. An uneasy realization of stupidity on my part gradually crept in as well.

How – I wondered – could it be missed? How did seven years in a country where people were more likely to faint at the sight of a microphone than speak into it, not prepare me for this? How could I fail to see the warning signs in a place where any public criticism of the regime was practically unheard of? And yet here was I eager to take to the airwaves and broadcast what was happening in Benghazi to the rest of the world.

In the heat of unfolding events some one thousand kilometres east of the capital, it had become easier to overlook various aspects of reality, things I should have known to be true. In that moment, Libya suddenly seemed extremely foreign to me. I was numb, confused and frightened.

THE BLOGS

Retrospective: Tripoli Residents "Quiet but Confused" 23rd February 2011

I had filed this rant – which we call copy – down a satellite phone line that day, unaware that it would be used in its entirety as a piece for Online attributed only to an unnamed witness. I had scribbled a few indecipherable notes on a piece of paper (later torn to pieces and binned) and phoned in to give the London team an update.

The idea was to inform the BBC at large of what was happening so – in my mind – another correspondent in neighbouring Egypt, namely my colleague Jon Leyne who was tasked with covering developments, could use some of the material or BBC Online could add snippets of the information to their stories. This was ultimately the birth of "Tripoli Witness", though, as you can see, not labelled as such at the time, and not nearly as polished as a written piece.

Despite the fears, just three days after the first massive anti-government protest in the capital that was brutally suppressed, there was an indescribable burning desire to file what I had heard from trusted friends.

Residents in Tripoli were in a daze, unsure of what to do next with the security crackdown and active campaign of fear meted out by the regime's forces. Meanwhile the state desperately wanted everything to appear "normal" as residents remained indoors and the entire city went into lockdown. Considering all this now, the regime's denial of events was almost as comical as it was scary. By then most expats and illegal immigrants were in the process of finding a way out of the country and locals felt trapped in what would morph into the cage that Tripoli became.

Tripoli Witness blog
23 February 2011

Tripoli residents "quiet but confused"

As anti-government protests in Libya continue, an eyewitness in the capital Tripoli gave this account to BBC News.

Tripoli is still quiet for the most part. Everything is still shut down and people don't really know what is happening. They are very confused.

Many are hoping that other people - anti-government protesters and troops who have defected - will come in from the towns or cities around Tripoli, to try to help residents here achieve something.

Let me tell you about some specific incidents that have happened here over the last two days.

"Bodies dumped"

In Fashloum, one of the poorest districts in Tripoli, and the scene of a very heavy crackdown, I heard an account of a drive-by-shooting.

It happened on Tuesday morning, when people were lined up to buy bread at one of the few bakeries that have remained open. Three people were killed.

There are also mounting accounts of what appear to be killings by paramilitary troops and bodies being immediately dumped in their trucks or cars.

There is evidence of shootings being cleared up - bullet shells being picked up and blood stains being washed off the street.

I heard of one such shooting in front of the state television headquarters on Monday afternoon.

Four people were killed and one of those was shot at point blank range.

Another witness told me of a similar scenario in Fashloum two days ago, when the anti-government protests first erupted.

I can also tell you about what has now become known as the "wild checkpoint". It lies about 12km outside the capital, at a paramilitary checkpoint stationed there.

They are pointing guns at people and making them get out of their cars. They are thoroughly searching the cars and questioning passengers. There have been some cases of interrogation.

"Mass exodus"

Banks and shops remain closed. But there was a text message sent out this morning to users of two state mobile phone networks.

It told everyone, civil servants and private workers, to go back to work.

In reaction to that text, one Tripoli resident, who works for a foreign company, told me:

"I don't understand how the government expects us to go back to work when there is a mass exodus of expats here and work is at a standstill because of the dangers of driving.

"There have been accounts of so-called pro-government protesters hijacking cars that have foreign number plates."

Another resident in Tripoli told me she hopes the people here don't go to work.

"This can be our way of peaceful protest," she said.

"We all stay home, civil servants and private workers indefinitely, and let Colonel Gaddafi and his sons run a ghost city. Let's see how long they last."

There are two Libyan naval vessels that have been sighted since yesterday, positioned sideways facing Tripoli.

People here believe they are gunships on stand-by.

• • •

Retrospective:
Trapped in the Libyan Whirlwind
2nd March 2011

It actually felt more like being "trapped in a cage" but with permission to wander out for good behaviour. People in Tripoli were quite lost by the time I wrote this, barely two weeks into the Libyan uprising. Their protests had not exactly yielded the results they did in the east of the country, which had managed to drive out security forces from there, and take matters into its own hands. They were uncertain as to how to go about defying the regime after the severe crackdown that saw men of all ages being picked up by security forces. The small town of Zawia, some 40 kilometres to the west of Tripoli was beginning to get pummelled into submission by the regime's forces after its residents staged massive protests and eventually managed to get some weapons to defend themselves in the process.

Colonel Gaddafi's regime had reversed into full denial mode. "Everything is fine, there is nothing" was the persistent claim by the regime's lackeys. A quick-fix some viewed as a bribe was introduced, a monthly $400 in cash for every family. This was ultimately a time when the government began an aggressive campaign to keep the capital quiet; many here perhaps underestimated its effectiveness.

They also miscalculated how difficult it would be to "rise" against the regime again and deluded themselves into believing it would take place every Friday, which only caused them a greater sense of frustration for many months to come.

With hindsight, it was premature to assume that the so-called "final battle" would be in Tripoli. Everyone believed it would be back then, and they did so until the day the Gaddafi clan and its security forces fled the capital in late August as rebels drove in from other parts of the country. Tripoli was a significant gain naturally; it allowed the new authorities to firmly cement their grip on power in the country.

Tripoli Witness blog
2 March 2011

Trapped in the Libyan whirlwind

I drove around the capital today to visit friends and stock up on more food for my family. We seem to have made a daily ritual of shopping for enough bread and staples to feed a small village.

"Just in case...," I'm told by family members. Just in case something happens and the supermarkets and vegetable stalls shut down indefinitely, that is.

It's quite evident we're not the only ones who are worried - the supermarket shelves are half empty during the day, although everyone knows that goods are abundant in the market this week.

There are quick, often muted exchanges of pleasantries between customers and shop owners.

People stare at each other with uncertainty. Although staring has long been a national pastime here, it comes with an air of distrust these days.

"Are you for or against? Are you armed or not?" Or, as I have found myself asking: "Where did all these young teenage men get all these new cars from?"

Things are far from normal here.

It appears that at least 80% of private businesses remain closed. People are either afraid of what each day might bring, or they have heeded calls by the grand cleric Sadeq Elgheriani, who appeared on al-Jazeera, telling residents to stay home in protest.

The only crowds you encounter are outside bakeries or banks, where people are collecting the 500-dinar ($400; £250) state giveaway to each family.

As I drove past one branch of BNP Paribas, a long queue outside its doors, a young skinny man in civilian clothes stood tall at the back of a pick-up truck, nonchalantly holding an assault rifle.

A few metres away, scorch marks blackened the concrete road. It's where anti-government protesters burnt things when they took to the streets.

Almost every main road that has any long stretch of wall bore the remains of graffiti in red or black with anti-government or anti-Gaddafi slurs.

They have been clumsily white-washed - what you see is a horizontal line of rather transparent white paint covering them - or at least trying to.

State schools are slowly re-opening, but several teachers say they are only going to work because they have to, and no pupils are turning up.

Wishful thinking?

It's the eve of 2 March, an annual public holiday marking Gaddafi's 1977 declaration of the so-called "people's power" system of government. Paradoxically, it was this declaration that many Libyans came to view over the years as the day they lost all power.

An infinite number of Libyan pundits based abroad have appeared on satellite news channels claiming there will be large anti-government protests all over the country; it remains unclear whether this forecast is based on tangible knowledge or wishful thinking.

Though this is likely to take place in what is now known amongst locals as the "liberated east" and parts of the western region, the capital still faces a challenge - the armed might of the regime's forces besieging it.

Libyan officials and state media have described the eastern part of the country as troubled, suffering, and taken hostage by al-Qaeda operatives.

However, events there are no longer under the dubious banner of "cannot be independently verified" or "amateur videos posted on YouTube purported to show".

Images beamed into most Libyan households in the past week have shown the tens of thousands - if not more - on the streets of Benghazi and other eastern towns, rejoicing in their newly-found yet fragile freedoms.

Brutal crackdown

Back in Tripoli, the scenario is starkly different.

There is a silent agony gripping some of Tripoli's families who have lost loved ones recently, or those injured by live gunfire who have refused to be taken to state hospitals, or those who have "disappeared" after detainment or death or injury.

I received a call from a dear friend the other day. Weary of the strict surveillance on the ground, online and on the phone, he only spoke of "minor" incidents in his lower middle-class neighbourhood on the night of Sunday, 20 February.

"In our street, two young men - brothers - both were taken away. They released one of them the next day, but the other one is gone," he said.

"Our neighbour at the end of the street was shot, but he's alive," he added.

That is arguably "minor" compared to the killings in the capital on the first day of protests - killings which people cautiously speak of only when they meet in person.

The government is still denying that there were protests in the capital.

The second time protests erupted in Tripoli was on Friday 26 February after prayers. It was small pockets of protests put down within a couple of hours. Shots rang out throughout the city.

A friend of mine told me of an incident in Arada Street, where a protestor was shot. As an elderly man attempted to help him, he was fatally shot in the head.

"Then a young teenager, not more than 17 years old, appeared from his building with a gun and started randomly shooting at the brigade forces, seemingly in an attempt to provide cover for the protesters as they dispersed," he said.

"The security forces quickly ran away, and so did the young man soon after," he added. "But within a few minutes, five vehicles with armed men appeared and started shooting into the air and at the tops of buildings there."

Another friend tells me he was sitting in a tiny cafe having coffee a few days ago, when a young man in his 20s turned up, pale and shaken.

He told the cafe owner that he went home to find that his mother and sisters were locked in a bedroom and his father forced to kneel on the ground as security forces raided their home.

The man lives in Souk el-Joumha, the scene of two anti-government protests here.

Residents in the Libyan capital remain uncertain of what's to come, caught in a whirlwind of change that hinges on events in Tripoli, where the so-called "final battle" is meant to occur.

• • •

Retrospective:
City of Fear and Silent Protests
10th March 2011

Shortly after the uprising began, and with the regime scrambling over itself to suppress the facts, I suddenly found that my mobile phone had acquired infinite credit. The government was paying for it, and for everyone else's. At the time, I didn't question why, instead I was simply elated that I had the perfect opening line for my next piece. It was ironic really; Libyans suddenly found themselves able to speak indefinitely at a time when it would have suited the regime better if they didn't speak at all.

The day before penning this next piece was the first time in three weeks that I had come into contact with Gaddafi sympathisers (not die-hard loyalists). Two of my mother-in-law's neighbours came to visit, and she lied about the whereabouts of her husband.

"He's in Cairo" she said. He was actually in Benghazi for family reasons, but any connection with the city where the revolution was then fermenting was not something to talk about openly.

Events in the country inevitably dominated much of the conversation which followed and my mother-in-law, sister-in-law, and myself, sat there nodding silently, feigning concern for the regime.

Hallucinogenic yoghurt? Poor old Gaddafi? We were so confused! I was taking mental notes, and silently praying they wouldn't ask what I did for a living. I had already indignantly decided not to say "housewife", as though being a career woman or not mattered at the time. I needlessly wondered, "Nurse?

Teacher? BA ticket saleswoman?" They never asked.

Months later, in July, one of them came back for another visit with a tall sprig of fresh rosemary, branches of bay leaves and a bunch of fresh basil from her garden. Over coffee and cake and out of the blue she said, "I've been seeing all these reports on Libya Al-Ahrar (a new channel at the time which supported the uprising) about Muammar's history and everything they say is true...I had forgotten what Gaddafi did."

At the time, Libyans who opposed the regime only shared their views with those they trusted, who were of the same inclination. On the other hand, people who supported Gaddafi's regime feared no one when expressing their political position. It was a reality that existed for decades but was compounded further during the uprising. As I write this now, the tables have turned for the first time since Gaddafi came to power in 1969.

Tripoli Witness blog
10 March 2011

City of Fear and Silent Protests

In recent weeks, the mobile phone service that allows users to check their credit has stopped working.

You now get a message saying "Unknown application" instead of the usual "Your credit balance is..."

Several people had already noticed that phone calls appear to be free - despite endless conversations, the credit never runs out.

In Tripoli, most are terrified to say anything on the phone that could be construed as resentment towards the regime.

Conversations are quick, short and of little substance.

So too are the lectures in schools, many of which have re-opened, although student attendance remains a trickle.

Private schools are facing a shortage of teachers - posts that were, until last month, occupied by foreign teachers, most of whom - if not all - have fled the country.

One of my family members - a 17-year-old who has returned to school - says she is not learning anything.

"We go to class, it's more than half-empty, and the teachers are secretly not teaching in protest."

Detentions and disappearances

But protesting in Tripoli is a dangerous business - the two times people dared to take to the streets here, they were gunned down into submission.

And ever since, there has been a sustained campaign of detentions by security forces who go knocking on doors.

Many detainees are released within two days, but - as one friend told me - "only after they take a beating and they have enough fear in their eyes".

Others simply disappear.

In one area of Souk al-Juma district, I heard that 120 men were taken last week.

Some young men now hide in safe houses offered by friends or acquaintances because "security people came and asked for me in my family home", they say.

Even residents who have family abroad, who spoke out on foreign news channels, have been arrested.

In the past three days, relatives and friends who have tried to leave the country tell me that they were asked by airport officials to present a legal document that states that they are "on vacation from work".

Those who claim to be unemployed will presumably be required to show an official document that proves they have registered "in search of work" with the labour office and that they have received the 150 Libyan dinars ($121; £75) in state aid that came into effect last week.

The limits on movement are tightening.

As flights out of Tripoli airport steadily decrease, many here believe that they will soon only be able to travel by boat or ferry - as they did back in the 80s and 90s.

New pastime

Not far away, in the town of Zawiya, residents and rebels have seemingly been bombed into submission.

Residents of the capital hold their breath in horror as they speak to relatives there - an increasingly difficult task.

Watching the news has become the new national pastime, as people venture out on a needs-only basis.

But the news is a source of increasing stress, bringing with it a sustained sense of frustration and helplessness.

"Why is it being described as a civil war when people are united, and the government and its hired forces are killing us?" people wonder.

But the capital is not united.

The city centre's Green Square has been occupied by pro-Gaddafi supporters - who opponents call the "paid traitors of the people's revolution".

Most are likely to be secret police, or members of the revolutionary guards and their families.

But, to the best of my knowledge, the price of fresh allegiance from average citizens came at a hefty sum of 17,000 dinars in cash, a new car and a lethal weapon - provided they pass some test proving their loyalty to the Gaddafi regime.

That aside, the media campaign being run by state television is gradually winning over the poorly educated.

They have expressed their belief in TV claims, such as: "The yoghurt brand, al-Naseem, is drugged."

This particular brand is owned by a family from Misrata, the port city under rebel control.

Or reports that: "The rebels are all al-Qaeda. Have you seen how they slaughtered our soldiers? We saw the pictures!"

"We just want to live in peace," another Gaddafi supporter says.

"Gaddafi is old now and he has been here for as long as we have been alive," an elderly neighbour complained. "The situation is breaking my heart."

Opponents of the regime would say the same, but for completely different reasons.

• • •

Retrospective:
Afraid To Watch TV
17th March 2011

It is quite incredible to read this piece and realise that it was written barely a month into the Libyan uprising. It was at a time when the residents of Tripoli were too afraid to watch what they wanted on their own television set.

You know there is a problem when you are trying to hide your viewing habits from the state. It sounds ludicrous but it was a distressing matter for many; for the families who were afraid their young school children would mistakenly mention Aljazeera, Alarabiya or BBC in public, or for the shop or cafe owners who did not dare switch from the state TV channels because they never knew who their customers were.

Looking back, I cannot help but wonder whether the state really cared. They probably did not, but managed to convince many that they did and that there would be dire consequences for watching the "enemy channel" or "channel of lies" as many a state TV presenter at the time labelled all the other news networks. I often sunk further into my seat and covered my face with both hands at any mention of the BBC on state TV; it was never to praise us of course. "Oh no! what about us now?" I would ask myself.

At that time most Libyan households were arguably glued to their sofas, constantly watching the news for updates on a country that seemed to exist in a parallel universe. Tripoli was slipping into a bubble of its own by then and many breathlessly and desperately awaited the results of a UN vote to impose a no-fly zone over Libya and approve a military intervention of sorts. Those in Tripoli who opposed the regime were not just afraid of every modern form of technology by then, they were arguably in fear of their own shadows and that of others they believed were watching them or their loved ones.

Tripoli Witness blog
17 March 2011

Afraid to watch TV

Every day at 1400 (1200 GMT) on the dot, our neighbour's 15-year-old son, Mohamed, delivers a bag full of bread to us: a ritual of "help thy neighbour" that seems to give comfort in these confusing and scary times in the capital.

He tells us he gets the bread for free because he has been volunteering at the bakery every day for the past three weeks.

Egyptians and sub-Saharan Africans once sweated in these local bakeries as they churned out loaf after loaf, but they have long since fled the country's unrest in fear for their lives - or are stranded at the airport seeking a way out. Now local residents have had to step into the breach.

Those of us who have stayed in the capital have quite a task ahead of us - not least of which is finding out what is happening in the city itself.

"Celebratory" gunfire?

There was heavy and sustained gunfire in Tripoli on Tuesday; it began just before 1500 and lasted a few hours. It's unclear where it was coming from; residents in the Gergaresh and Gurji districts said it was particularly loud there and they took cover behind closed doors.

The standard government explanation is "it is celebratory gunfire and fireworks" - but we can't understand why what sounds like anti-aircraft artillery is being used rather than the usual festive fire from Kalashnikovs.

Information is coming through at a snail's pace due to heavy surveillance of modern communications.

Many local businesses have even reverted to fax machines to communicate with the outside world. The internet has been shut down for almost two weeks now.

On the ground, people and families only exchange tales when they meet in person.

It was not until Wednesday night that I learned from a relative, and later several friends, that there had been an anti-government protest in Gergaresh on Tuesday afternoon - explaining the gunfire.

As for the claims made by the Libyan opposition abroad of a fighter jet suicide attack on Col Gaddafi's Bab al-Aziziya compound that evening - it's unlikely, but who knows? The rumour around town is that some even saw smoke rising from the compound.

Fake smiles

I visited an old friend earlier this week.

His son arrived home from university shortly after we sat down for an afternoon coffee.

When I asked him how his studies were going, he replied: "I was standing talking with a friend on campus just before I left the university and this girl we know came up to us and loudly announced that al-Jazeera and al-Arabiya news channels had been erased from their channel list because she and her family only watch one "true" channel, al-Libiyah [the state-owned one].

"We just silently nodded with a fake smile and said our goodbyes."

There is disappointment in his voice as he carries on: "I can't believe she is so blind - you think maybe she was pretending because there were people watching us there?" he asks.

His father and I knowingly shook our heads like ageing wise men but could offer nothing in response.

It's not only university students that are feeling the stranglehold.

Several primary school teachers recount similar stories of young pupils being questioned by school employees aligned to the regime's Revolutionary Committee Movement, which is being used to suppress dissent.

The conversations they have with these children, as young as eight years old, are along the lines of: "How are your parents? Are they sad about what's happening in the country? What have they been saying? What news channels are you watching at home?"

All, it seems, in an effort to establish whether the students have parents or relatives that are potentially opponents of the regime.

Back at my friend's home we briefly switch channels to watch the state-run al-Libiyah. There's a man on the screen "confessing" the error of his ways to the Libyan leader in what appears to be a tent.

My friend tells me of a report he saw on the channel, warning the public of "cars being rigged with bombs in crowded areas" - by the ever elusive al-Qaeda elements in the country, that is.

"This means the regime is going to start doing that," my old friend concludes.

As I sit back and write this, the neighbourhood children are playing along the dirt road in our area - one of hundreds of streets in the capital that have been left unpaved over the past four decades.

I can hear one of them chanting "Al-Fateh! The people's revolution! Al-Fateh!" in reference to Col Gaddafi's 1969 revolution.

Children are being taught to chant these words in public, and for good reason.

Words not only play an integral role in the regime's fight against the international community and its own people - they can also determine the fate of entire families.

• • •

Retrospective:
In Fear of Gaddafi's Secret Police
21st March 2011

Having travelled and worked in some of North Africa's worst dictatorships, I have always found the term "secret police" inappropriate. They are not a secret when you know they are everywhere. Libyans did not only fear the "secret police"; they feared their neighbours, their friends, and in some cases a relative, a sibling or even a parent.

This was especially the case in Tripoli. The capital is composed mainly of outsiders. They come from Sirte – Gaddafi's hometown, from Misrata in the west, from Benghazi in the east. This mix of backgrounds, values, and allegiances provided a serious obstacle to the formation of a popular opposition movement in Tripoli. Most did not really know or trust each other enough to believe that if they were to organize or take part in a protest in their district, they would not be let down by an informant in their midst. Outside Tripoli, communities were smaller; people knew each other well.

In Tripoli during the uprising, many residents were rounded up for detention either because an informant had filmed video of them protesting, or because someone they knew or who lived in their area had given them up. Others were simply taken away for the purposes of intimidation. That was why, after two substantial attempts to begin protests in Tripoli, most were forced to give up.

It was the districts that largely housed the original families of Tripoli – the Arab Tarablous – that dared stage defiance at every opportunity; Souk el-Joumha, Fashloum and Tajoura – they all knew each other there. However, even then, it did not make them immune from arbitrary arrests and fatalities.

Tripoli Witness blog
21 March 2011

In Fear of Gaddafi's Secret Police

A sense that "time is not on our side" is running through the city, not just for opponents of the regime but also - it would appear - for the regime itself and its devoted legion of supporters who seem available around the clock to take to the streets and wave posters of Col Muammar Gaddafi, or "offer" themselves as human shields at his residence.

When the UN resolution for a no-fly zone was adopted, the regime's opponents in the capital - and there are plenty of them - were rejoicing at home - away from the eyes and ears of the informers and secret police deployed across the city.

"Finally," one said. "When will they start implementing it?" another impatiently cried.

It didn't take long. As I write this on a chilly Sunday night, I can hear a barrage of anti-aircraft artillery being fired. It was a similar scenario on Saturday.

Word travels fast

As we watched the news channels report on the missile strikes by the US against a military defence target near Tripoli, several friends in different parts of the city told me they saw ambulances driving around the city in circles - seemingly aimlessly - with their sirens on.

They believe the government was attempting to cause panic among residents here and "give the illusion that there are casualties somewhere".

Not surprisingly perhaps, we soon saw reports on Libyan state TV claiming dozens of civilian casualties.

I recall a time when the mood on Arab streets - not least in Libya - was one of anger and disbelief at reports of civilian casualties at the hands of US strikes in Iraq and Afghanistan.

In contrast, I found myself surrounded by people here scoffing at the local reports.

"They are lying. We would have heard by now if there were any civilians hurt. Everyone knows everyone here, and word travels fast," some said the next day.

"So, the regime has finally made use of the dead bodies they gunned down here and then snatched from streets and hospitals," another one offered.

The men of Benghazi

There is a joke circulating amongst Tripoli's men: "When Libya is liberated, our brothers in Benghazi will march to the capital with containers of women's underwear to distribute to us."

They collapse in laughter as they tell the tale and sip on their coffee.

At least one woman in Tripoli has expressed a similar view, but this was no gag, as far as I'm aware. The incident was witnessed by my relative's friend at a bank in the Souk al-Jumaa district.

An old woman, in her late 70s at least, I'm told, entered the bank to collect her 500 Libyan dollars ($410; £253) in state aid announced a couple of weeks ago.

There were two long queues - one for men and one for

women. She stood in the men's queue.

The men urged her to move to the women's section. "Why?" she challenged.

A man told her: "Ya haja [a term of respect for an elderly woman] this line is for men, women is the other one".

She loudly replied: "No. All the men are in Benghazi."

The room is said to have been stunned into silence and she remained in her place until her turn came and she walked out with her money.

It is perhaps a bittersweet private reminder of how frustrated many here are at the lack of efforts in Tripoli in recent weeks to defy the regime and take to the streets.

However it is also placated by the fact that they did try - twice - and were met with a force so brutal that they conceded it was simply a suicidal task. There is considerable anger brewing behind closed doors here in Tripoli.

Beaten and kicked

My friend was detained earlier this week by armed men, for no apparent reason.

He was blindfolded and taken from a location that will remain undisclosed for his own safety.

He says he was detained by members of the fiercely pro-Gaddafi Khamis brigade.

"I was shoved into the back of a Land Cruiser and every time we approached what was probably a checkpoint they would shout at the security officers manning them to 'move away'."

He was held for 24 hours and then released.

He was taken to two detention centres; the first one a prison in Ein Zara on the outskirts of Tripoli - where he spent the night - and the second in Salaheddine the next day where he was interrogated.

"I was beaten on the back, kicked around when they threw me on the floor and slapped countless times during interrogation," he recounts.

"There was at least 100 other men - young and old - in both facilities I was taken to, not just Libyans but Egyptians too.

"I could hear people shouting and screaming. One of the men around me told me he was from Zuwara and asked that I try to get the message out to his family there that he is alive - if I were to be released."

There were also two brothers being held there, he recalls, and one of them was blind.

"They said that their father was killed during the protests in the Souk al-Jumaa district and they were picked up from their home and brought to the prison in Ein Zara two weeks ago," he says.

Sombre mood

My friend was ultimately lucky - he got out - while others continue to just disappear after detention with no information available to their families.

My relative tells me of one of her friends. Her husband has been missing for two weeks now, he is 62 years old and was picked up from their home by men in plain clothes.

We hear stories of this nature almost on a daily basis.

It almost seems like everyone knows someone who has been beaten, detained for a day or two or "disappeared".

Three hours ago, I learnt that another friend of mine from Tajoura district has been detained since Friday.

I learnt this through a mutual friend who I went to see in an effort to lighten the sombre mood that has plagued most residents of the capital the past month.

Mission not accomplished.

• • •

Retrospective:
Fear and Uncertainty
26th March 2011

At the time I wrote this, we were uncertain of how to refer to my identity; I was a genderless being writing for BBC Online.

What would become a full-on petrol shortage was just beginning and Nato's airstrikes had become a comforting reality to many in the capital – including the household I lived in. The sentiment was a shared one on my part, though I recall privately questioning whether it was right for me to share that reaction given that I am a journalist; it is an issue I struggled with for many months.

I had experienced worse in my short lifetime, like an Israeli bombing raid in south Lebanon in the mid 1990s; we would hide in bomb shelters back then, but in Tripoli, most people were just curious and not afraid. Most welcomed it as a sign that somewhere in the skies someone was protecting us and they secretly hoped it would kill the Colonel.

There were countless times my husband, his brother, his sister and their slightly ageing petite mother excitedly raced up the stairs of the house and out onto the roof in the dead of night to try and make out where the bomb hit. It was a mass stakeout for a plume of smoke in the distance – mostly. The young men in the neighbourhood were almost always on their rooftops as well – a scene repeated across the capital.

The regime tried to paint a skewed reality against the Nato airstrikes – they tried really hard! Now that I have Internet around-the-clock at my leisure again and having gone through the abundant supply of commentary by anti-war advocates and campaigning journalists available on the web, I look back and wonder if I missed something. I did not.

Tripoli Witness blog
26 March 2011

Fear and uncertainty

Who ever thought that an oil-rich country like Libya could face fuel shortages?

That is exactly what is happening as I write these words. People - including myself - have been scrambling to fill up the tanks of their cars in anticipation of what appears to be a looming threat of fuel shortage - or even worse - no fuel at all.

It is one of the few reports on state television you can take at face value. It is also physically visible in the long queues at petrol stations across the capital.

My relative and I spent two hours waiting our turn on Thursday, and in the end we succeeded only because the manager is a friend of a friend of a neighbour. As instructed, we reversed into the petrol station from the exit end and shamelessly re-fuelled as others stared us down with visible disdain.

I never thought I would live to see the day where you needed "connections" to get petrol here. My friends in other parts of the city tell me many stations are closed for business, which fuelled even further panic.

Whistlers on roof

A new public talent is on display these days.

Every night in Tripoli, since the coalition air strikes began, people race to the rooftops of their buildings or houses at the first audible sound of anti-aircraft artillery shots or the rumble of an explosion.

A few minutes in, you will start hearing the men whistling, some are close, others from a distance, and - in the otherwise still and silent dead of night - the chorus of whistling echoes across the neighbourhoods and rises up.

No-one really knows what the whistling means - we're left privately assuming that there is an underlying tone of excitement in the choir and not of the type that would impress the regime.

Another new talent being enforced is stone-throwing. I have yet to see it for myself, but my friends excitedly tell me of the scenes they witnessed.

"Some people in Ben Ashour area and in Souk el-Jumaa district have been stoning the pro-Gaddafi, green flag-bearing cars that drive down their streets; they throw the stones and sprint," they say.

"Lollywood"

However, it is not just opponents of the regime displaying new talents.

Some would argue that the country's state-owned television channels have recently lifted the "iron curtain" on directors and actors who have long been absent from the scene.

They marvel at the footage being displayed claiming there have been civilian casualties in coalition air strikes in Tripoli.

There was one scenario on Wednesday night that seemed particularly suspicious. It showed one woman - with only her back in view shouting and screaming over the debris.

This was accompanied by other short scenes of security

officials closing the doors of an ambulance and telling the driver to go. Look closer and you will notice the faintest of smirks edging across the face of one of the emergency personnel.

The scenes on television of the funerals have also come under scrutiny. What stands out the most perhaps is the absence of emotion - usually a key element of any funeral here.

"They are making a mockery out of death... this is like an inferior version of Hollywood. It's Lollywood!" one friend says in disbelief and anger as he watches the screen.

There is still no clear picture on whether there have been any civilian casualties as a result of the coalition strikes; but there certainly hasn't been any talk of any on the streets of Tripoli amongst the people.

Death is very public knowledge here: under normal circumstances, residents are not only told of people who have died in Tripoli - whom they have often never heard of - but even in cities farther afield.

The dozens of civilian casualties being claimed by the government would hardly go unnoticed.

"Group torture"

A friend of mine recently released from detention - where he was severely beaten - described the conditions in one prison facility, where he says hundreds of Libyans from Tripoli, Misrata, Zawiya and Zuwara were held.

"They have a tape that replays 24 hours a day in the cells on loud speakers - the audio of Col Gaddafi's first televised speech after the start of the uprising where he says he will 'sterilise' Libya house-by-house, street-by-street," he says.

He goes on to recount how security officers used what he believes were stun guns in one room where they carried out "group torture".

"We were all lined up against the wall and one security officer came in and shocked the detainees as he walked along - it was random, he somehow missed giving me a hit. I was still blindfolded and all I could hear was the sound of an electric shock and the men making a restrained painful sound through clenched teeth and falling to the floor.

"I kept praying in hushed tones. In the cell where I spent the night, there were countless men who told me they had been there for days or weeks, most were wearing pyjamas - which suggested they were dragged from their homes late at night - and many had urinated in their pants."

He saw families: one elderly man and his three grown sons for example, who were brought in because the fourth son had been grabbed during a protest in Tripoli on 22 February. They have not seen him since.

• • •

Retrospective:
Humour amid the Fear
31st March 2011

It is, perhaps, part of human nature to look for humour in our darkest hours; many Libyans did so for decades under Colonel Gaddafi's rule. The lighter side of the Libyan conflict was a common theme in Tripoli Witness's features. At the time I wrote "Humour amid the Fear", finding something to laugh about was a necessary form of escapism from the harsh realities on the ground.

We were almost two weeks into Nato's bombing campaign. Many misguidedly thought – or rather hoped – the regime would collapse as soon as the West intervened and that the rebels would suddenly make very significant progress on the frontlines. Instead, the running battles between Ajdabiya and Brega in the east of the country were beginning to look like a stalemate, which confounded many here.

Some Libyans in Tripoli had just begun to lose hope that the armed struggle would yield any results at all. My husband and his family on the other hand were still religiously watching television with the constant hope "tomorrow" would bring good news. For them and many other families who were natives of the eastern region, and cities in the west like Misrata where battles were raging, it was personal! They were caught in the capital, which was not their real home, but they could do nothing to help oust Gaddafi at that point. They had to just sit and wait.

A glimmer of renewed confidence amongst many emerged with one of the most high-profile and surprising defections from Gaddafi's inner-circle, coupled with the tragic experience of a

Libyan woman which implanted a new fear amongst Tripoli's residents.

Tripoli Witness blog
31 March 2011

Humour amid the fear

It rained in Tripoli for much of the day on Wednesday, which not only dampened the dust and sand of this city, but also - it seemed - the mood of many people here.

They are feeling increasing pressure from shortages of fuel, money and bread.

But as night fell the news of Libyan Foreign Minister Moussa Koussa's defection to the United Kingdom left many here breathless.

For those who have been nervously watching scenes on their televisions of the rebels advancing then retreating over and over again, the sense of a stalemate that could prolong the conflict has been gradually sinking in - rather depressingly.

For those opposed to the regime, Mr Koussa's escape from the country seems to have instilled fresh hopes; they believe that the regime is on the brink of internal collapse.

One friend likened the foreign minister's departure to "the colonel losing his spinal column".

This resignation is unlike any of those witnessed since the uprising began six weeks ago - it is the most significant yet.

He was not merely a minister; he is one of the most feared personalities in the country - the "man of death" as he is locally known - and one of the most trusted figures in Col Gaddafi's inner circle.

Some would argue that the Libyan leader trusted this man more than he did his own sons.

The now ex-foreign minister of Libya was the chief of the country's notorious external intelligence service for 15 years.

"Mentally ill"

Before the civilian uprising here, the handful of anti-government dissidents who dared speak out publicly against the regime were immediately branded by officials as mentally ill and subsequently detained indefinitely. It's a tale that Libyans are familiar with.

It is therefore not surprising to many that Iman al-Obeidi was immediately described by officials as mentally ill last week after she stormed the hotel where the foreign media have been confined and said she had been raped.

The images of her being dragged away by security and silenced as journalists trying to defend her were beaten has struck yet another fearful chord amongst residents here.

What is new in this instance perhaps is the claim by officials that she was intoxicated.

She is not the first case of rape we have heard of here.

I have heard of two other cases in recent weeks. One of them was of a Moroccan housekeeper who was left behind by her employers as they fled to a safe house because half their family members had been detained.

The story that circulated through word-of-mouth was that security forces stormed the house she was staying in with the intention of detaining the rest of the family. Finding her alone there instead, they raped her.

The news reports we have seen say that Ms al-Obeidi said she was targeted because she was from Benghazi - a revenge attack by pro-Gaddafi forces.

That too is not the first case to be heard of here among Tripoli's residents.

There have been several incidents in different parts of the capital branded as revenge attacks, where prominent families originally from Benghazi have apparently been targeted, their homes raided, searched, and their laptops and mobile phones taken.

In one instance, a security officer told a family: "You Easterners, 'hay aleikon hey [a local expression to convey a warning]'."

Intoxicated

My friend recounted what could be regarded as an amusing scene he witnessed from his balcony in downtown Tripoli more than a week ago.

"It was late at night and an elderly man wobbled his way down the street shouting 'Allah [God], Muammar [the colonel], and Libya!' He paused for a moment and turned to a group of men standing on the street and added: 'But he [Muammar Gaddafi] IS taking long isn't he? He said it will be over in days, no?' It was quite a sight!".

There were fits of laughter - I'm told - from the group of men listening to him as they gently urged the drunkard to go home. What is odd in this scenario is that up until a month ago, no man in Libya publicly displayed intoxication - not least because alcohol is illegal here.

Libyan inspired "Possible Scenarios"

Every day analysts abroad - both Libyan and foreign - have been spinning possible scenarios for Libya's future.

Residents of Tripoli have come up with a set of their own fictitious and humour/terror-based outcomes that are far from the traditional outlook. These are just a few of what I've come across in recent weeks.

- If the coalition air strikes overtly go after the leader himself, Col Gaddafi will press a secret button in his bunker which will detonate bombs across the country and wipe it off the map.

- If the regime regains control of all of Libya it will dig a very large hole, put all the opposition in it and burn everyone alive.

- The leaders of the opposition in Benghazi are secretly regime loyalists. They will reveal themselves soon and we will discover this was all a big lie.

- The Libyan leader and his sons will face the public and the world, apologise for all their wrongdoings and ask for forgiveness.

That last one usually draws a roar of laughter in small circles. It may seem impossible to find humour in times of war and fear - but it happens.

• • •

Retrospective:
Covert Protests and Black Humour
14th April 2011

Libyans are nothing if not always up for a good joke. During Gaddafi's rule, their sense of humour could be dark indeed. It became a way of criticizing the government, without doing so overtly. Creating a joke out of a depressing, confusing or even deadly event was – for decades – their quiet protest. But only in private, of course.

The Colonel himself seemed to have mastered the art – only in public. As he faced the biggest threat to his regime, he made his shortest public appearance in history. It was less than one minute on state television, at around 2am on the morning of February 22nd. He was seated in his golf buggy and looked like he was ready to board a plane to Moscow; with a black leather and fur ushanka on his head, a matching jacket, and holding an oversized white umbrella above the vehicle's roof. All this to declare he was still in Libya "not in Venezuela", as rumours suggested. "Do not believe the channels belonging to dogs", he said.

At the time this next piece was written, covert protests and small acts of defiance were taking place across Tripoli. Reading this now, I can see they were largely futile in comparison with the war raging elsewhere in Libya. However to residents in Tripoli, these "small acts" kept the spirits of the regime's opponents alive.

Tripoli Witness blog
14 April 2011

Covert protests and black humour

Thursday is the eve of the two-month anniversary of the Libyan uprising that kick-started in Benghazi on 15 February.

Someone, somewhere has called on residents here to fast on Thursday as a sign of solidarity and protest against the regime.

Looking at the pictures of what is now an armed struggle and full-scale war between the government's forces and the improvised rebel army, it is easy to forget that this revolution started peacefully - albeit for the first three days.

The way of the gun here is not so easily forgotten, however, and there was on Wednesday night an incident which was a reminder of why and how this became transformed into an armed struggle.

"Arada district is in an uproar," a short phone call reveals - this is code for "people have taken to the streets and are being shot at".

For now we do not know exactly what happened there on Wednesday night and are unlikely to find out for another 48 hours. Over about half an hour, we frequently heard gunfire - and it was no ordinary firepower being used.

There was a sudden burst of gunfire close by. Peering outside the gates of our home, we saw many in the neighbourhood doing the same; we silently mouthed to a young man across the street, "Where is that sound coming from?"

Much to our horror, he shouted back, pointing to a street behind us: "It's coming from that dog from the Revolutionary Committee Movement [the regime's security and ideological arm] who lives down there! He's shooting into the air!"

Wide-eyed and shocked at the attention-grabbing response, we gestured for him to be quiet and swiftly went back behind closed doors, eventually to be engulfed by the silence of night once more.

Out of paint

There is a fine line between humour and reality these days. There are a couple of bleak examples of black humour making the rounds in Tripoli that are probably inspired by real-life accounts.

The first goes like this: "Some of those being detained here by security forces are being driven around for hours then abandoned on a road because there's no more space in the jails and detention centres."

The story, which is told with a baleful smile, is likely to remind some people of their own experiences. One of my friends detained last month can probably relate.

He told me: "When I was taken, the vehicle they transported me in made the first stop, but the people in the car were told by a voice outside: 'There is no space here, take him to Abu-Salim [prison]'. We must have driven there because the next exchange was 'No, no it's full here; go to Ein Zara [prison]!' We got off at the next stop and I was dragged in."

Though he was blindfolded the entire time, it was these stops and exchanges that shed light on where he was being taken.

The other grim gag is slightly more colourful: "Tripoli has run out of paint - the regime has used up the last of its reserves in its repeated attempts to whitewash the anti-government slogans across the city's walls."

This was probably inspired by the cat-and-mouse game

evidently still being played by opponents of the regime and security forces. It's not quite Banksy, but let us call it artistic urban warfare.

In fact, some Libyans unable to write on walls outside are now doing it inside.

The latest trend was demonstrated in a public school for girls - the Quortoba High School in Hay el-Andalus district. Word quickly spread about what happened - "it's the talk of the entire neighbourhood", a friend tells me.

You would be forgiven for thinking this next illustration of artistic expression is a joke, but it is not.

Red, black and green helium-filled balloons have been spotted rising into the capital's skyline on several occasions in different parts of the city.

The colours represent the original post-colonial flag of Libya that has become a symbol for opposition-held territories here. Reports suggest that when they can, security forces shoot the balloons down.

"Property of the enemy"

Back in the 1980s and mid-1990s, when the regime identified its opponents, it was common knowledge that on some rare occasions their homes would be demolished; a sign to residents in the area that an opponent had been rooted out.

Old habits die hard and it appears this particular one has reappeared in the year 2011. A house was knocked down in the up-scale residential area of Ben Ashour, somewhere behind the Souk el-Mourjan, a friend tells me.

The rumour is that it was "housing the enemy".

Meanwhile, in the commercial and residential district of Gergaresh, I'm told an oil service company residence -

owned by a man who is apparently out of the country and appeared on a news channel condemning the regime - was raided, ransacked and wrecked.

Although crimes like theft have been on the rise in recent years it appears their incidence is now widespread.

A large number of foreign companies have been the target of looting in the past month. The foreigners - who made a quick exit from the country at the start of the uprising - left behind offices, and quite often their civilian security guards at the gates to keep an eye on their properties.

The guards speak of how security forces accompanied by armed men in civilian clothes are leading the raids on these assets; when that happens, company cars, computers and anything remotely valuable are taken along with them.

Some abandoned Arab embassies - including, last week, the UAE embassy - have also recently suffered a similar fate. For added measure their flag was taken down and replaced with the green flag to declare it government property.

Colour - it seems - is of the essence these days in both sides of this conflict.

• • •

Retrospective:
Tales of Defiance and a Mystery Man
21st April 2011

Every random act or "tale" of defiance against the regime was seen as a new thread of hope that Tripoli was not being left behind in Libya's mass revolt. To many in the capital, these acts restored a sense of inner peace and kept many entertained – a bit like popping a few Xanax pills I imagine. There were other similar stories in the months that followed, after my column "Tripoli Witness" was forced into silence and long before the capital fell. My favourite was the one of the fruit and vegetables salesman who arranged his produce in the colours of the "new" flag. Aubergines were used to reflect the black, tomatoes for the red, and lettuce for the Green. Unfortunately for him, his fleeting act did not go unnoticed.

At the time, state television – the regime's mouthpiece – was in full gear. In reality it confirmed much of what we heard in its attempt to intimidate the population into submission. Every day it spoke of things that shed light on realities on the ground. "Don't watch or listen to those enemy, colonialist channels" they often warned.

In case some of the regime's opponents thought their silent protests had gone unnoticed, there was a special show which focused on accusing businesses of failing to work properly or of being closed when they should be open, anything that suggested the workers were not wholeheartedly behind the regime. The presenter would then issue a threat suggesting the accused business would be taken over by "other people who will do the job". All things considered, Gaddafi's regime was its own worst enemy.

As the months passed, Tripoli seemed unable to shake itself into conclusive action. It was like a patient in a persistent coma. The eventual recovery was seen by many in the city as a miracle.

Tripoli Witness blog
21 April 2011

Tales of defiance and a mystery man

I have come across some interesting and amusing analogies for this conflict in the past week.

"The opposition is singing along to the tune of 'Hit the road, Jack', while the regime's ruling family rocks on to the tune of 'Should I stay or should I go'," one musical analogy goes.

Another is: "It's like a bad round of poker. The winning hand is bluffing until the last minute when he reveals his true cards, but his opponents around the table are well aware of the ruse throughout the game."

Realities are not as light-hearted, however.

Last Thursday afternoon, a friend of mine stopped by to tell me what he had seen and heard.

"There was a small anti-government demonstration by students just outside Nasr University. I heard the shooting because I was in the area, I walked over and got as near as I could and I saw a crowd and a scuffle," he explained.

"Then security forces moved in, sealed the area and pushed out onlookers. We all left quickly. Other people I know later told me they saw some blood being covered with sand. No one died, but someone was definitely injured in the shooting."

Dark threats

To a visitor - not that there are many these days - and to some looking from the outside, things may appear normal here. But the reality is far from it.

For example, every TV screen in cafes, clothing stores and mini-markets is tuned into the same state-run station that no-one really watched two months ago. In normal circumstances, they would be beaming out al-Jazeera Arabic or a music channel.

"We can't change the channel," a shop-owner tells me. "The security people randomly check all our shops to make sure we don't put the 'enemy' channel on."

That is not the only tale from private businesses. Many tell me they were forced to open their stores and cafes, having shut down for two weeks following anti-government protests in Tripoli on 20 and 25 February.

"Remaining closed was our way of protesting, but they [government entities] told us we have to open or they would give our shops to someone else and they will continue our business," one said.

Others tell me of a darker threat by various security apparatuses. "They said: 'You open or we will destroy you and your family and your shop.' So what can we do?" another said.

All these measures are arguably adding pressure on many here who are already reeling from the state of limbo they find themselves in.

"Gone mad"

Most grown men and women are pestered by their families to return home before sundown - the unspoken civil curfew.

It is perhaps understandable, given the unwanted trouble

that can be caused by the sporadic gunfire (not against Nato aircraft) that often envelops some parts of the city at night, as well as the countless checkpoints that emerge on every street.

Tripoli resident

But daylight is not necessarily a pleasant experience either.

A friend told me about his cousin who - last Monday - said she would go mad if she stayed at home for another day.

"She went out and took her mother with her. It was around one in the afternoon. As they drove up the main road in Gergaresh they were forced to slow down as three cars sped past them.

"There were two white Chevrolet cars chasing another car with a young man driving. They quickly cut him off and forced his car to pull over.

"The men in civilian clothes who jumped out of the two white cars were armed with Kalashnikovs. The two women saw the men dragging the young man out of his car by force; they beat him, tied his hands together and threw him into the back of one of their cars and drove away.

"My cousin made a quick U-turn and came back home terrified of what she saw."

My friend is visibly uncomfortable as he recounts the incident: "That was in broad daylight! They don't care who sees what any more, it's like they've gone mad and are constantly out for blood," he adds.

Hooded man

In the Souk el-Joumha district, one of three large areas in the capital that are home to many of the uprising attempts, there is a "talking wall". In a fit of laughter my friend recounts a story his friend witnessed in four consecutive days because he lives close to the infamous wall.

"At first we saw an anti-government message painted on the wall: 'May the regime be toppled.' Then we saw it white-washed - [presumably by local neighbourhood government agents] - and written over in black: 'Allah, Muammar [Gaddafi] and Libya.' Then we saw that message white-washed and written over with an anti-regime slur. It went on back and forth like a conversation for three days until the last message we saw said: 'NO! We told you, No! - Muammar only!'"

Then we have a mysterious figure that has emerged on the streets recently.

There is a hooded man, I'm told, who runs around in public in Salaheddine district.

"Every time there's a Nato air strike in the capital, he runs around a street shouting: 'May the butcher [Colonel Gaddafi] fall! May the regime be toppled!' And then he flees. I don't think he's been caught by anyone yet. We still hear about him," a friend tells me with a thoughtful grin.

Meanwhile, there have been several sightings of the "opposition flag" in Tripoli, albeit for a fleeting moment.

A friend of mine who lives in Salaheddine district saw one flapping about in the wind early one morning last week. "It was on the roof of a small clinic next to the mosque," he amusingly recalls.

Another flag - quite surprisingly - was briefly raised on top of the Taqadom School in Ben Ashour district, some residents there tell me.

A stolen moment of "freedom" here comes in different forms, in an attempt to let off steam from a city that has been likened by many here to a sleeping volcano.

• • •

Retrospective:
Rioting, Fighting and Dying for Fuel
28th April 2011

Aside from the chaos, the fighting, the endless queues and the occasional deadly incidents, there was an element of twisted entertainment in actually witnessing what happened at your average petrol station during the uprising. In late April 2011, two months into the Libyan conflict elsewhere in the country, I had begun a ritualistic sleepover once a week at a friend's home.

We could not visit each other often or casually meet up for brunch or coffee on the other side of the city because we were watching the fuel tanks. The only obvious solution was to spend the night and make the visit worthwhile; in 24 or 48hrs, we could have our lunch, dinner, coffee, and cake without making countless trips in the car and spending our precious fuel.

Her home overlooked a petrol station that was eventually completely shutdown as the fuel crisis deepened.

One night in May around 2am, the station opened after 24hrs of closure and a desperate queue of "sleeping cars" were suddenly alive again. The arguments began as the queue pushed forward. Tempers flared. A group of about 15 men at the entrance of the station argued with one of Gaddafi's soldiers in their midst who seemed to be even angrier. As the cursing and shoving intensified, an assault rifle was raised by another man in uniform standing a few metres away from a car that was happily refuelling. He fired into the air and the rifle was spitting out orange sparks in the process. I watched the scene like a peeping tom through a sliver of an opening in the shutters of a dark kitchen window. My friend had strictly instructed me not to turn on the lights because "they can see you if you do". It was not a time you wanted to be caught staring at a chaotic scene.

It did not appear to occur to anyone that the shooting could blow up the station and a good chunk of the surrounding, heavily populated area, including my friend's home. I could not budge; it looked fascinating! It is odd how one's ideas of entertainment transform when there is little to do or little that is seen. Sabrina – my friend – laughed at my engrossed state of-self when she checked in on me some fifteen minutes later. I secretly wished she was delivering popcorn.

Tripoli Witness blog
28 April 2011

Rioting, fighting and dying for fuel

It has been an explosive week in Tripoli, both literally and figuratively.

Nato air strikes intensified after a quiet period.

Meanwhile, the fuel shortage, that state television channels deny exists, has hit an all-time high in the past eight days.

The shortage has not only lasted longer than people expected, but it has also sparked everything from mini-riots to gang fights and, incredibly, shootings as well.

State television announced that as of today - Thursday - we may only have fuel for the amount of 5 dinars ($4), no more, no less.

It has instructed stations to stamp car registration papers with the date of purchase because we can now only refuel every three days or more.

The only official explanation for the shortage has been that, while there is a surplus of petrol, some people are panic buying and others want everyone else to think there is a fuel shortage and are creating long queues to trigger chaos.

I have seen the longest queues at petrol stations that residents here have ever witnessed.

Some will stretch and wind through several streets in residential areas, others are up to 2km long - at least the ones I have seen.

Friends will swear passionately that they have seen others that are much longer.

It is by all measures a sad and miserable sight. The experience of acquiring fuel is not only dismal, however - it can also be frightening, hazardous and lethal.

There are those whom we can call the coalition of the unwilling - a minority group in Tripoli that would rather not queue for days and nights for petrol.

They are patiently waiting for the fuel crisis to be somehow resolved. Others it would appear, have invested in bicycles.

But for the majority of the capital's population it is a different story.

Deadly Encounters

My friend successfully re-fuelled his car on Tuesday after three long days and nights in a queue at the petrol station in his area.

Resilience and planning are key.

He and his brother queued in shifts - they would alternate every three hours during the day and every five hours at night.

He, like many others in the queue, was desperate. His wife is pregnant and due any day now.

"I can't afford to be short on fuel in my situation," he explains.

At that petrol station and many others across the capital this week, fights have been breaking out sporadically between people.

This is the account according to one witness:

"One night a massive fight broke out. People took out knives and others phoned their relatives telling them to come help with the fight. It quickly spiralled out of control. At least three people were stabbed and we heard that one of them later died from his wounds. There have been similar incidents at many other stations."

Meanwhile, my friend who queued for three nights witnessed other incidents.

"On one day some cars tried to create a second queue. The brigade forces threatened them, shot into the air and shouted. Some left and others stayed.

"Twenty minutes later several cars arrived filled with civilians resembling criminals. They had chains and metal bars and immediately attacked the cars that had refused to leave.

"They smashed the windshields, mirrors and hoods and then got into their cars and disappeared as quickly as they appeared. The security forces just watched."

On Tuesday morning at a petrol station in Abu Nawas on Gergaresh road, "there was a drive-by shooting targeting the queue. Two people were killed. The cars were white

Chevrolets", another friend tells me.

He did not see it happen but his friend witnessed it.

Yet another friend tells me, at the petrol station along Ghorji Road this week, "a riot broke out and security forces moved in immediately and tear-gassed the crowd".

"I was caught in traffic there because of the chaos and almost choked on the tear-gas," my friend said.

Dangerous dialling

The security crackdown in this city remains a vital tool for the regime in almost every aspect of daily life. It is an ever-present reminder of the conflict that has so far been staved off in the capital.

A chaotic scene and a mobile phone is probably one of the most hazardous combinations these days.

On Saturday night a friend witnessed a shooting on Sidi Masri road.

"A fuel tanker, parked on the side of the road, was illegally filling a few cars with petrol. There were a few brigade men securing the perimeter as this took place.

"A car carrying two men pulled over close by, on the opposite side. One man got out, crossed over and started video-recording with his phone. The security forces saw him and called out: "You! What are you doing?"

"He started running away and they shot him. We saw him fall. Immediately the car he came in drove off. There was a taxi near them - the driver was probably working for internal security because they told him to follow the car and he sped off in pursuit. The man who was shot was picked up and thrown into the brigade force truck. They drove off with him."

It is not surprising to hear of the dangers of being caught with a mobile phone in your hand that appears to be filming.

Another friend also witnessed a similar incident at a petrol station queue in broad daylight.

"A teenager standing in the queue at the station held up his mobile phone and appeared to be filming the chaos. I had a feeling it would not end well. I looked over to where security forces were standing and saw one of them watching him from a distance.

"The young man put his phone back in his pocket and turned away. As he did, the military man sprinted, slid over one car and grabbed him from the back and put a knife to his throat.

"He shouted at him 'Give me your phone! Where are you going?' Then he spoke into his hand-held radio and a civilian car pulled over. They threw him in and drove away."

In Tripoli these days, petrol is arguably not only a fuel for cars but also a fuel that is igniting the much repressed anger and, some would argue - confrontation - between residents of this sprawling city.

• • •

Retrospective:
Mourning, Protests and Opposition Cats
6th May 2011

It was more like an opposition barnyard quite frankly. Other tales that later emerged included stray dogs, chickens and pigeons. Images of any of these animals were difficult to find. But a week after I wrote the article a friend managed to get me a seven-second video, recorded on a mobile phone, of a man's arm trying to control a pigeon that had the "opposition" flag tied to one of its legs. It was from a "friend of a friend" – in Tripoli – and shot indoors before it was presumably set free to antagonize the authorities here. We laughed at these acts at the time; they were quite amusing – though desperate by all measures.

Back then one could not help but wonder what others in the country were thinking of their "brothers" in Tripoli. Many Libyans had joined the war by then, firing live ammunition, and most residents in Tripoli were excitedly discussing the latest animal used in their covert acts of defiance against Gaddafi's regime. They were worlds apart – a reality that is evident even now, months after the fall of the capital as Libya's new forces feel that Tripoli did not "participate as much as other cities or regions in the conflict". Those in the capital genuinely felt they were pushing the limits, however small and insignificant they may seem today. By then there were rebel volunteers who fled the capital to join the battle on the frontlines elsewhere and some risked their lives smuggling videos, pictures or information on USB sticks or hard drives across the border into Tunisia.

What many did not know at the time was that there were other underground "operations" in Tripoli that could easily be depicted in a Hollywood blockbuster. Weapons were beginning to get smuggled in through the sea and some were readily available at a high price in the black market that seemed to exist somewhere near the earth's crust. Tripoli was slowly, but surely prepping for its own eventual uprising that was to be cemented by incoming fighters from other parts of Libya.

Tripoli Witness blog
6 May 2011

Mourning, protests and opposition cats

The killings of one of Colonel Muammar Gaddafi's son and al-Qaeda's leader have been the subjects of many a social or family gathering over the last week, but only after everyone complains about the continuing fuel crisis.

Some here see Osama Bin Laden's demise as a message from the Americans that "now we are free to come after you [Col Gaddafi]".

The government announced that Saif al-Arab Gaddafi and three of the colonel's grandchildren were killed during a Nato air strike on one of the ruling family's homes.

The initial reaction from those who support the regime was obvious to see on state television.

Those in the capital with a lesser opinion of the ruling family reacted in stages.

Conspiracy theories

At first they were stunned.

Then they were sorry because that particular son was regarded as a figure who was far removed from the regime and someone they knew little about.

You will often hear people say these days that he was "God-fearing, conservative and rumoured to have been opposed to his family's handling of the conflict... and his eldest brother Muhammad is the same".

The third and final stage was scepticism.

"They're lying. None of them died, the regime only wants to gain public sympathy," sceptics now argue.

Minor details like the lack of images showing the faces of those who were buried, or doubts that the entire family would casually hold a gathering under one roof in these uncertain times have fuelled that theory.

We have heard officials here "apologising" for the attacks on some European embassies by the angry mobs who were protesting against the coalition strike that killed Saif al-Arab.

However the accounts of witnesses who gathered close by when the havoc broke out before dawn on Monday tell a different story.

"Stolen chairs"

There are numerous accounts of the brigade forces and armed men in civilian clothes storming the embassy grounds and setting the buildings on fire as bus- and car-loads of people arrived to loot to their hearts' desire.

"I saw one woman running out with a baby pram and a children's plastic swing," one witness said.

Others saw everything from refrigerators being hauled out, to bottles of alcohol being fought over.

"The brigade forces took some [bottles] as well and put

them in the back of their trucks," another witness said. "I even saw them taking plastic chairs."

However they also say they saw public security police teams looking uneasy and trying to control the chaos outside and inside these diplomatic premises.

"They were the only official apparatus present that were not participating in the looting," I was told.

There does not appear to be any end in sight to the fuel shortage that started to hit Tripoli 14 days ago.

You have two main options to refuel: Spend an average of three nights of your life in a queue or get someone else who has connections with the station to queue for you.

You pay him a 50 dinar ($42, £25) fee for the rationed amount, which officially sells for five dinars, and he promises to get it for you within 24hrs.

A third, less advisable option, is to buy a 20-litre container of fuel from the black market, only to discover it is mixed with water when your engine starts to smoke.

And after witnessing, on several occasions, military guards firing their Kalashnikovs into the air to disperse a fuming mob less than 10 metres from the rare working fuel pump, I feel compelled to suggest that all petrol stations put up a big sign saying: "WARNING. Approach at your own peril, station may explode."

Gaddafi tent burnt

Over the last seven days my friends have told me of several incidents they have witnessed or been told about.

It seems immediately after an intense Nato bombardment, there were small anti-government protests in different neighbourhoods in the capital.

There was also the burning of a pro-regime Bedouin tent in the Hadba district; a few of these tents, symbolically associated with Col Gaddafi, have been set up in the capital in recent months.

Even animals have been drawn into this conflict.

There have been several sightings of stray cats parading around with the opposition flag painted on their bodies.

Some, I am told, were unsuccessfully chased and shot at by angry security agents and secret police who work in the Souk al-Joumha and Janzour areas where they have been seen.

Unanswered questions

A week ago, there was a confrontation between Souk al-Joumha residents and security forces.

A friend of mine who was in a small grocer's shop in another area that afternoon overheard an exchange between an elderly woman talking to her son over the phone.

He phoned and told her not to come home and to go and stay at a relative's place nearby.

"Why? What's going on?" she cried out in a panic.

Her son told her there was a lot of shooting and that it was not safe to return.

When she hung up, the owner of the shop asked her what was wrong and if he could help and she told the story.

It was not clear what the clashes were about as it is not a detail that can be relayed over the phone these days.

Unanswered questions over "minor" incidents like this and the greater news events of the week are what is on the minds of the people in this capital these days.

Retrospective:
Tribalism and the Threat of Conscription
13th May 2011

An entire volume should be dedicated to Libya's tribal debate. During the uprising, there was no shortage of pundits in the West speaking of the dangers of tribalism in Libya and painting an apocalyptic scene of how this "issue" could play out in a post-Gaddafi Libya. It was an utterly misguided analysis at the time, even before Gaddafi's regime played the tribal card.

It was also inaccurate to say that the late Colonel unified tribes here – he tried to repress them for decades, afraid that if any of the country's big tribes wielded too much power, it would be enough to topple him. Libya was historically divided along regional lines, Tripolitania, Cyrenaica, and the Fezzan federal states. When the Colonel came to power, the states had already been united under the former monarchy of King Idriss. Though tensions remained between the west, east and south, they were exacerbated by Gaddafi. The eastern region particularly felt marginalised. The war arguably helped unify them as they fought towards a common goal and faced a shared enemy.

In the dying months of the uprising there was an attempt by the regime to undo decades of tribal knots. It was a last desperate move to try and galvanize support for the Colonel. That left behind the bitter knowledge – for those who fought against the regime – of the "tribes that stood by him". It may have simply been a last resort but one cannot help but wonder if there was more to it; did the Colonel secretly hope that if things were to turn for the worse his legacy would be tribal fractures that would take years to heal?

Tripoli Witness blog
13 May 2011

Tribalism and threat of conscription

You know there is a problem in a country when you find that almost everyone you know is awake until the dawn call to prayer - and afterwards sleeps from sunrise until the early evening before sitting with their families again with nothing much to do.

The exception to the boredom is the still-worrying situation of fuel shortages, and a new phrase - "tribal allegiances" - being hammered out on state television.

The paradoxes of life here are on the rise and it is no longer only through official rhetoric.

In the country that spent decades battling the influence of tribes, there appears to be a concerted effort by the regime to revive their role.

Many watched the national conference of Libyan tribes on state television this week with an inescapable degree of confusion and at times amusement.

They gathered to propose solutions to end the bloodshed, among other aims that were arguably lost through the pro-government rhetoric that dominated the discourse of most speakers.

"Who are these people?" was a common first reaction.

"Since when do we have a national tribal council or whatever they call it and since when do we speak in the name of tribes?" was another.

A common conclusion offered was: "This is it, the regime is sowing the seeds of tribal rivalry, by making them all think that he is giving them power".

Rising unemployment

We all have a lot of time on our hands these days and we spend much of it watching television or discussing what we have see on our screens. There is a reason for that.

The closures of foreign companies, along with some well established private local ones, have been problematic for many people.

They now only exist in name and spirit and in most cases with a green flag waving in the gentle breeze on the roof of their headquarters, while armed security agents idly sit outside the gate on a plastic chair, sweating beneath the Sun's rays.

This has significantly increased the already high unemployment rate that existed in the country before the uprising.

It could be argued that the law requiring all foreign companies to employ a majority of Libyans has now paradoxically created more unemployment.

The foreign companies seem unlikely to ever come back or resume activity so long as the regime remains in power - or at least as long as their countries insist they want a change of government.

Tens of thousands of educated men and women found themselves unemployed overnight in the early days of March.

It is perhaps no wonder that many people - particularly in the capital - have been growing increasingly restless.

Dangerous dilemmas

Over in the state-run companies, it is a different story.

There is undoubtedly support for the regime among the ranks of civil servants, the majority of whom have long been employed by the state despite having few qualifications, in an attempt to ease unemployment.

These are the people who stand to lose a lot in the event of the current regime's exit.

There are other civil servants in the capital, however, who are equally adamant that anything less than the complete downfall of the regime is unacceptable.

In late February they stopped going to work - mainly out of fear of what would happen following the anti-government protests.

"We were contacted by our bosses insisting we come back to work," someone who works for a state-run company told a friend of mine recently.

"They penalised us through our salaries for every day we were absent. At the time I felt that if I were to resign I would endanger myself and be branded an 'opponent of the regime'.

"I and other colleagues returned to work with a plan to quit within months to avoid raising any eyebrows. I am resigning soon and will probably leave the country when I do."

Civil servants are not the only ones who are looking for an exit.

In the past week talk of military conscription took a very serious turn after months of rumours and elusive references to it on state television.

All public sector companies in Tripoli were given official notice of the military draft plans through a letter carrying a message that was to be passed on to all male employees.
A civil servant told another friend of mine of the developments in a panic-stricken tone that made us all nervous for various reasons.

"We've been informed that the first conscription phase is for those between the ages of 20 and 40 years old and for those who have completed military training between the years 2000-2011."

As a man, you are required to do this training at some point in your lifetime.

However what you find here is a mixed bag of men who faked medical reasons to get out of military training, men who have not done it at all, men who have false official documents saying they trained when they have not and men who have actually done the training.

News of the conscription has so far prompted some men to make a quick exit from the country to avoid it. Others are making arrangements to leave as soon as possible.

Three months ago, no-one here ever imagined they would find themselves in this precarious situation.

Those civilians opposed to taking part in attacks on their fellow countrymen now face a dilemma.

Either they take the risk of leaving the capital or they stay on and face being forced to fight their fellow countrymen on behalf of a government they silently denounced long ago.

• • •

Life in Hiding
26 August 2011

It is a refreshingly cool August night with a gentle breeze that - in my mind - is gently sweeping away the anxiety, frustration and fear that has reigned over this city in the last six months. Or dare we say over this country over the last 42 years?

The neighbour's wall has had a recent makeover, with the new flag - the pre-Gaddafi monarchy flag - painted on it, and a message stating that "Libya is Free".

Six nights ago, that would have been white-washed by the state and many a home would have been raided to track down "the rat" who did it.

I have been reporting for the BBC from Libya for seven long years, but have been "off air" for six, much slower, months.

As Facebook pages calling for a 17 February protest in Libya multiplied by the day, so too did the concern.

There were sleepless nights of fretting over how to report on a protest given the circumstances. Being one of just two foreign correspondents based here and being newly wed to a Libyan from Benghazi made for what seemed like a lethal combination - an arrest and "disappearance" waiting to happen. [Many families from the east and from Misrata were persecuted for regional affiliations.]

In the early hours of 15 February the mobile phone rang at about 02:40. "Private number" flashed on the screen and my heart seemed to jump to my throat. I knew it had started and London was calling.

Fear and isolation

Benghazi's residents phoned with minute-by-minute

updates and by 07:00 I was broadcasting off-and-on, as and when the fear of the consequences of doing so consumed me and subsided. I was still the only one reporting the story from inside the country.

Two days on, it was nightfall again and the panic reached a pinnacle.

My husband reminded me we were not in Benghazi, and that in Tripoli someone would come calling. The exchange was riddled with a sense of fear, isolation and tears of helplessness and frustration on both sides.

"They have a death brigade that specialises in people like you, I can't help you, no one can!" he warned. "They will knock on our door and drag you out in front of me and execute you! You have no idea what they are capable of. What will I do?! Tell me!"

The next day my mobile number was blocked.

I stopped broadcasting, got a new number and waited. On 20 February our neighbour, a man from Gaddafi's hometown of Sirte who worked at the now wrecked Bab al-Aziziya compound, crossed paths with my husband in the building's stairway.

"So your people aren't going to keep quiet?" he asked, nonchalantly. We packed a small case of belongings and all my broadcasting equipment and left to stay at my in-laws' home.

That was the night Tripoli's unarmed residents staged their own massive, peaceful protests.

It was also the night that the sounds of heavy artillery and gunfire that met them ripped across the city.

Mental lifeline

I was broadcasting again for TV and radio as it happened -

that is until Col Gaddafi's son appeared on state TV some two hours later as a re-invented character - a hardened, threatening figure who took everyone by surprise. Tripoli soon went quiet.

That was the last night I broadcast out of Tripoli - up until six days ago that is - due to a combined concern from senior editors in London and myself over safety.

When I was called to attend a news conference the day after the first of the protests in Tripoli, I informed authorities here that I was taking a career break for personal reasons.

"Life in hiding" is an uncomfortable term to use because I was not physically chased by anyone; just by the demons of paranoia at the simple knowledge of what might happen.

It is perhaps an inevitable consequence of living in a dictatorship for many years.

There is no doubt in my mind that as a British-Lebanese foreigner, I would have - at best - been thrown out of the country if I had continued reporting on that fateful night and the days and months that followed.

That, and the possibility that my husband and his family would have been held responsible for my actions and could have been dealt with in unimaginable ways.

That is how "Tripoli witness" was born. I was to write as a man - to quell any suspicion of identity - who could not be named. For three months, these entries served as a mental and physical lifeline.

But they had to come to an end.

As the months went by, gathering information became increasingly difficult. Many friends and sources fled the country - some after fears of imprisonment and torture grew for a variety of reasons.

What was life like for Tripoli Witness, backed with incredible moral support from editors in London, over the last six months?

Months 1-3:

Jumping out of bed at all hours of the night, every night, at the sound of any movement outside, and thinking: "This is it, they've come to get us, they've tracked me down knowing I'm Tripoli Witness" - or worse: "They've come for my husband's family because they are from Benghazi and they'll raid the house and accuse them of being 'spies' when they find my broadcasting and communications equipment."

Baking a cake every three days when the stress felt too much to bear.

Growing an unusual predilection to trashy romance novels found in a friend's book collection.

Being told every Thursday night each week that Tripoli will rise again "this Friday" and our edgy existence would come to an end.

Dreading phone calls from concerned family and friends abroad, mainly due to paranoia that they would say something offensive to the regime and because there was little I could say except, "everything is great, we're fine, Tripoli is peaceful and everything is 'normal'". (All phones were tapped and people were being detained on the basis of the recordings.)

Months 3-6:

Same as above though some practices dwindled due to supplies.

Being ever so grateful that two girlfriends remained, and that I saw them once a week in a sleepover involving a cook-off, DVDs and endless conversations about our lives and the country in candlelight and under a starry night sky.

Misguidedly taking up knitting for several weeks before realising it would never be a career option or even a hobby.

Having frequent disturbing dreams that often included Col Gaddafi and people being executed.

Questioning whether it was "time to leave" this miserable existence because it might drag on for years.

Deactivating Facebook account due to concerns it would be hacked.

Experiencing sheer elation upon finding the best hiding place for all the broadcasting equipment.

Above all, an increasing fear of my own thoughts that could not be hidden, and gradually wondering if this was the beginning of a mental breakdown. It was not.

• • •

EPILOGUE

20TH NOVEMBER 2011

There are many stories on Libya and of its people that remain untold and there many more to come as the country paddles its way into unchartered territory.

I have often been asked why I moved to Libya as a correspondent when no one else did or could at the time. At 22, back in 2004, it was not bravery that brought me to Tripoli, it was sheer naivety and good timing.

Gaddafi's regime had just started "opening up" and I imagine as officials stared at my application to move to their country as a correspondent, they thought it was the perfect opportunity to show just how "open" they were and allowed me to come in. I cannot help but wonder if they felt it safe because I was young and inexperienced at the time.

Many years on I was asked why I remained in Libya. In all honesty, the reasons changed throughout my time here. At first it was because my father diligently reminded me that I was a "Jawad" and that we do not just "give up" when we are afraid. That was his standard answer during my first few months in the country, as I sobbed through tales of intimidation from the state authorities, daily hardships, and all-around exasperation at trying to get a story out.

My mum would at times grab the phone from him and say "come back, just leave!" as she sobbed along with me. I didn't leave.

My father's reaction was a far cry from his original thoughts on my posting.

"Libya?! You're going to Gaddafi's Libya?!...Gaddafi with his crazy hair and those scary bodyguards around him...No!" he said the night I broke the news to him of my imminent travel plans.

As the months and first two years went by it was stubbornness that prolonged my stay in the country. The more I sensed the regime was trying to scare me into giving up, the more determined I became to remain a thorn in their side. Three years on it was the people of Libya and their stories that kept me there, as well as the friendships I gained. There was always a persistent nagging voice in the back of my head that said "there's more to do." There was.

Obscurity suited the atmosphere I worked in. I trod carefully and avoided doing TV because it was monitored by the powers that be more often than radio and that is where part of the significance of the BBC World Service lies for third world countries and dictatorships. I could have – long ago – done an earth-shattering piece on Gaddafi's regime, which would have simply had me thrown out and probably raised my profile. But what would be the point? I chose to stay to give people here a voice, which they had not had in decades. In doing that, the conventional views on the purpose of journalism were inevitably re-defined in my world. My work probably only made a difference to those I spoke to; I'm painfully aware of that and beat myself up for it for years, and continue to do so.

By the fifth year, when I seriously contemplated a move elsewhere in the region, I met and fell in love with a Libyan man who is now my husband and the rest, as the say, is history.

The present and future of Libya are as uncertain and unpredictable as natural disasters. Colonel Gaddafi, the dictator for more than four decades, is dead but his shadow lingers like a menacing presence. Many here believe that it will soon fade, but it will take time.

There is a power vacuum that needs to be filled but we have yet to see any worrying signs that everything will suddenly collapse or that a new Afghanistan, Iraq or Somalia is on the horizon. I believe it is largely due to Libya's small population and the overwhelming majority that struggled and fought for a common goal – to topple a tyrant.

Libyans are at the precipice of a new beginning and the fall will either be cushioned, painful or deadly. The most likely scenario in my mind is that it will be painful.

As a journalist, I believe Libya is facing extraordinary challenges. Muammar Gaddafi constructed and left behind a nation void of any viable institutions, any laws that are respected, or any structure of governance to build on. The Colonel, his family, and the former regime's henchmen refused to go down without a bloody and bitter fight to the end, which left a trail of destruction and lingering hatred and bitterness between those who supported the 2011 popular uprising and those who either rejected it or were indifferent to it. The war has also made way for new rivalry between the country's regional brigades in the absence of a swift installment of a transitional government. That is the Colonel's legacy in the country he vowed to live and die in.

The fear that long ruled people's lives has vanished though and today Libyans can openly raise their worries and discuss their differences on the future they are striving to create. The country's new state media is now a questioning tool to reckon with. Libyan officials are no longer paying lip-service to one man and his ideology; they now have a country and a population's needs and demands to answer to.

If it all fails it will not be Nato's fault. I would also argue that it will not entirely be the fault of the new authorities with the enormous task of maintaining stability in a post-conflict and post-revolution Libya and seeing it through until a constitution is formed and elections are held. This is the Libya that Gaddafi left behind, one that appears tremendously difficult to build. But it's not impossible.

As a bystander witnessing the birth of a new nation and the hope of a people who now dare to dream of better days to come, I cannot help but share their anticipation.